Garrison Town to Commercial City

St. John's, Newfoundland, 1800 to 1900

Compiled and Edited

by

Ronald Rompkey

DRC PUBLISHING
3 Parliament Street
St. John's, Newfoundland and Labrador
A1A 2Y6
Telephone: (709) 726-0960
E-mail: staceypj@nl.rogers.com
www.drcpublishingnl.com

Library and Archives Canada Cataloguing in Publication

Rompkey, Ronald
Garrison town to commercial city : St. John's, Newfoundland 1800 to 1900 / Ron Rompkey.

Includes bibliographical references and index.
ISBN 978-1-926689-44-9

1. St. John's (N.L.)--History--19th century. I. Title.

FC2196.4.R66 2012 971.8'1 C2012-900803-6

Layout and design: Becky Pendergast
Cover photo: Robert Pilot, "Sunrise, St. John's Harbour, Newfoundland," Oil on Canvas. Courtesy of The Rooms Provincial Art Gallery Collection.

Published 2012
Printed in Canada

We acknowledge the financial support of the Government of Canada through the Canada Book Fund (CBF) for our publishing activities.

We acknowledge the financial support of the Government of Newfoundland and Labrador through the Department of Recreation, Tourism and Culture for our publishing activities.

Contents

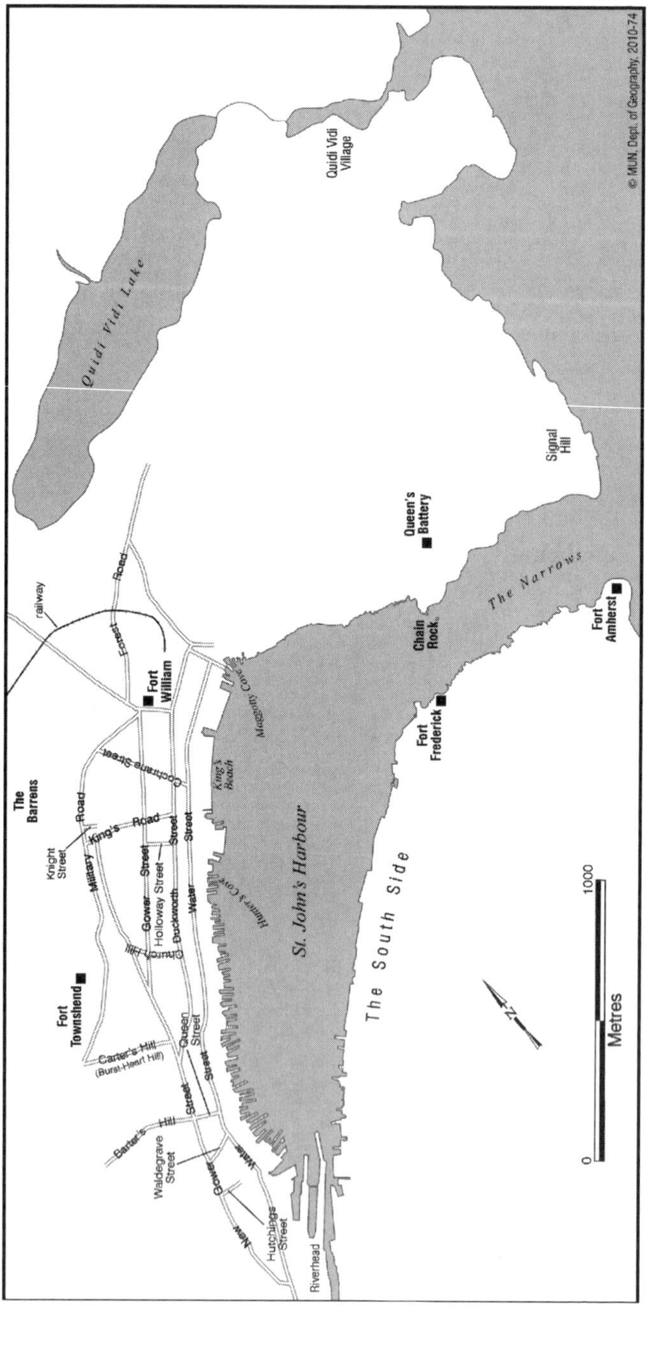
Quidi Vidi Lake
Quidi Vidi Village
© MUN, Dept. of Geography, 2010-74
Signal Hill
Queen's Battery
The Narrows
Fort Amherst
Chain Rock
Fort Frederick
railway
Forest Road
Fort William
Maggotty Cove
King's Beach
Cochrane Street
The Barrens
Road
King's Road
Knight Street
Military
Street
Street
Gower Street
Holloway Street
Duckworth
Water
Hunter's Cove
St. John's Harbour
The South Side
Church Hill
Fort Townshend
Queen Street
Carter's Hill
(Burst-Heart Hill)
Street
Street
Carter's Hill
Waldegrave Street
Gower
Water
New
Hutchings Street
Riverhead
N
0
1000
Metres

Preface

In this volume, we engage with local writers and visitors in St. John's, Newfoundland, from 1800 to 1900, a time when it emerged from its status as a garrison community and took on the characteristics of a more industrialized city. These writers recount significant events that contributed to a sense of community in St. John's, and thus I have chosen articles that present a collage of styles and perspectives that give the reader a taste of life as it evolved throughout the nineteenth century. To make these more accessible, I have occasionally altered spelling, punctuation and paragraph structure and added explanatory notes.

For their assistance in locating and copying these articles, I am grateful to Joan Ritcey, Head of the Centre for Newfoundland Studies at Memorial University, and her staff. I am also grateful to Charles Conway for cartography. Finally, I thank the Provincial Archives of Newfoundland and Labrador for permission to publish extracts from the papers of H.F. Shortis and Wakeham Pilot of Montreal for permission to use Robert Pilot's "Sunrise, St. John's Harbour, Newfoundland," as a cover illustration.

R.G.R.
Department of English
Memorial University

Introduction

The capital of Canada's newest province, St. John's is a modern city comparable to any other Canadian agglomeration of its size. The same commercial products abound, the same transportation is available and the same media of communication. Moreover, it is the site of the largest university in Atlantic Canada. Yet there is also a sense of timelessness. The fog still enshrouds it, the surf beats incessantly at the cliffs and the tide returns like clockwork. In order to enter the port from the Atlantic, it is still necessary to maintain a steady bearing of 276 degrees. Yet cities, like people, change their identities in the course of time, and St. John's is no exception. Inhabited some years after John Cabot arrived in 1497, it has evolved throughout the centuries. Where the capacious harbour once protected numerous wooden vessels, as well as ships of the British and French navies, steel-hulled fishing boats now tie up at a new basin constructed near the entrance, and the jetties secure the red-hulled ships of the Canadian Coast Guard, as well as service vessels supporting offshore oil rigs, container ships and the occasional cruise ships bearing foreign tourists. The downtown core described herein has since been surrounded by extensive suburbs, and the streets abound with commuters.

As Alan G. Macpherson has demonstrated, the port entered the historic record in 1519 and served as an industrial base for the migratory fishery for a century thereafter. The first record of permanent settlement, he shows, is a reference to houses already built in 1627, and we get our first view of the beginnings of a community 42 years later. A list of inhabitants from 1703 lists 79 ship's masters,[1] and during the winter of 1754-55, there was a dramatic increase from 80 to 212. That number continued to climb to 260 before dropping to 90 in 1759-60 but passed 400 in 1774-75. Over the next four decades, the numbers rose rapidly and passed 2,100 in 1828-29. Thus, the census for St. John's and Quidi Vidi in 1794-95 reveals an occupational structure still dominated by fishermen but also by a coterie of merchants.[2] Towards the end of the eighteenth century, British army personnel also constituted part of the community that continued to flourish into the early nineteenth century. Thus, from 1800, a series of historic events produced a sense of solidarity that would form the basis of the permanent population.[3]

We begin in 1796 with an article from *Lloyd's Evening Post* that lays out the extensive military establishment, as well as the growth of permanent settlement and the hostile visits of the French. Next, Sir Robert Pinsent describes the military force of 600 men and the living conditions of the small settlement of 3,420 at the beginning of the nineteenth century, as well as the carriage road cut through the forest on the south side of Quidi Vidi Lake called Forest Road, resisted by some as an unnecessary improvement. At this early stage, the town had already begun to change, as shown by the dwellings, retail shops, public houses and gardens situated in the lower part of the town where fish flakes had formerly stood. We also learn in 1804 of the first project for making a regular street outside Water Street so as to accommodate artificers, shopkeepers and others not directly connected with the fishery. Governor Gower permitted a road to be marked out about 200 yards from the high-water mark, and it was afterwards named Gower Street.

The commercial culture in early St. John's is demonstrated by an amusing tale related by Bishop M.F. Howley to demonstrate how, in the early decades of the nineteenth century, St. John's had begun to consolidate itself with a population of 10,000 and further immigrants pouring in, principally from Ireland, bringing with them elements of their own cultures. When the American war broke out in 1812, fortunes were made from unusually high prices, and St. John's became the base of operations for the British fleet. In relation to this, H.W. LeMessurier relates the arrival of Elias Durnford of the Royal Engineers in 1809 and the discomforts experienced by British soldiers. And an article from *Colonial Commerce* gives us a picture of daily life in 1815, as well as the economic changes that took place after the Battle of Waterloo.

We are then shown the devastation of the first of three fires that marked St. John's in the nineteenth century, each one more devastating than the last. In this case, the fire began on Water Street and continued to the west, then to the east, so that a considerable part of the western half of the town lay in ashes. As well, H.F. Shortis describes in compelling detail how criminals were brutally and humiliatingly punished by being hanged, flogged, placed in the stocks, paraded through town with labels on their backs or sent to Australia. In John Baird's geology, the Scottish geologist sets forth in great detail the rock formations surrounding the community and their colours, as well as the quality of the soil. This is followed by an account of a Beothuk woman seized by a fisherman in order to receive a reward of fifty pounds offered by the government to anyone who could bring in a Beothuk alive. This captive was treated with great humanity by the population, but the fisherman later murdered her to possess the gifts she had received. When we come to 1836, Bishop M.A. Fleming recounts the tribulations of a Roman Catholic missionary engaged in supplying sacred texts to his parishioners, as well as the ravages of a smallpox epidemic and the difficulties encountered in building a church in Petty Harbour and carrying out other episcopal functions.

We then learn from the Rev. John Brewster the effects of the second conflagration, the fire of 1846, and the devastation to follow. Next, there is a remarkable account by H.A. Emerson of a project to harvest wheat in 1848 initiated by Governor Le Marchant, accomplished by turning untilled government grounds into wheat fields and dispelling the myth that Newfoundland soil was unsuited to farming.[4] H.F. Shortis then turns sociologist as he details St. John's social life in the 1840s and 1850s. Here he divides the town into two distinct classes: fishermen, mechanics and store clerks on the one hand and the "quality" – an exclusive circle of army officers and their wives, government officials, legal and medical professionals, shopkeepers and civil servants – on the other. He also describes their styles of dress and the way in which electoral campaigns were carried out after responsible government.

In the first account shown here from the pen of a visitor, the writer identified only as "Portia" relates the discomforts encountered during a sojourn of three months. "The place," she tells us, "is at once filthy and picturesque." The streets, according to her, were narrow, ragged and tortuous, opening into quarters of unimaginable filth, tumble-down hovels, windows with broken sashes, decrepit fences, streets paved with old rags and decayed cats and other animals. The town was so hilly, she notes, that pedestrians walking on level ground proceeded as though going uphill. A second visit from Boston in 1870 is recounted by the American author and diplomat S.G.W. Benjamin. Benjamin describes with great irony the antics of certain Newfoundland passengers of Irish origin and their belief in the supernatural. St. John's had by then a population of about 23,000, and Benjamin found it to be a cross between an Irish and an English town where the streets abounded with dogs, "almost as if it were a Turkish city," some of them burdened by a billet of wood about the neck that rendered them harmless. The port, he finds, was sheltered, crowded in summer with vessels of many nations, so that on entering the harbour one was struck by an "ancient fishy smell." Yet poverty seems to have been the rule among many ordinary citizens, for the fishing industry remained under the control of monopolists who exploited the truck system.

The third great fire occurred in 1892, and we learn from the *Dominion Illustrated Monthly* that the distress was widespread. This fire, A.C. Winton informs us, began at five o'clock in the afternoon of Friday, 8 July, on the upper west side of the harbour and was driven downtown by a northwest wind that swept the slopes densely covered with houses. He also provides details of the extensive support in money and goods supplied by various Canadian cities. The same fire is evoked poetically by Eros Wayback (pen name of St. John's poet Edward St. George). And H.W. LeMessurier conveys the difficulties imposed on daily life by showing the lengths required to bring out a newspaper in a town virtually destroyed.

In 1897, the New England writer Edward G. Porter writes of the 400th anniversary of John Cabot's arrival. Since the voyage of Cabot in 1497 had become by then the founding fiction of Newfoundland, he is surprised to find that Cabot himself had not been publicly recognized, even though the British had done so in Bristol. Part of the reason for this, he imagines, was the lack of definitive documents and charts associated with the voyage and with the life of Cabot himself. "And so," he writes, "it has come to pass that we have not a scrap of information about either of the Cabots in their own handwriting; and in the general confusion, we are left with only what others have said and written about them – and that almost exclusively about Sebastian." He describes the memorial tower built in Bristol, as well as the Halifax proceedings of the Royal Society of Canada devoted to the Cabot quatercentenary, attended by guests from different parts of Canada and some older universities and historical societies of the United States. However, he does not neglect the fact that on the "broad carriage-road leading to Signal Hill" there was laid the cornerstone of the Cabot Signal Tower, which he describes as "a massive structure to be built of rock quarried on the spot." He continues, "There are two veins, purple and blue, which will be used alternately. The square, two-story central hall is flanked by square, castellated towers, one for a signal station and the other for an observatory. The lower story is to have thick battering walls, the roof will be battlemented and the flanking towers armed with bastion lookouts." Although it was not built on the scale described here, the tower remains a prominent marker to this day.

The same year, a taste of the growing commercial life in St. John's is evoked by the *Christmas Review* in its account of the Water St. firm of Martin Bros. that traded primarily in lumber but also sold hay, oats, potatoes, butter, meat and poultry. A visit to their stores, we learn, would reveal piles of turkeys, stacks of geese and ducks and mountains of mutton, beef and pork. Also, the spread of organized sport, as the town grew, is revealed in an article on rugby published in *The Record*. Here we learn that the principal opponents of the local team were soldiers or visiting seamen aboard British warships. However, the writer assures us that local interest in the sport was growing rapidly, even if there was no permanent, enclosed ground for games to be played.

The St. John's journalist P.T. McGrath sums up the status quo at the end of the nineteenth century in an article published in *Nash's Pall Mall Magazine*. The town, he tells us, had survived the great fires of the century and had now reached a population of 30,000. "They form a race of brave, hardy, generous people who," he writes, "in their isolation, have preserved the noblest virtues of the race from which they sprang, unsullied by contact with the great world outside." Moreover, St. John's was now the site of the principal station of a new railway system with a trunk line running through the interior of the island and terminating at Port aux Basques, where the steamer *Bruce* provided daily communication with the continent. Likewise, steamers were available to take the traveller to any part of the island and to Labrador. H.F. Shortis also testifies to the progress evident in

1899. The old streets now featured sewerage and electricity, with supplies of pure water. Water Street was lined with stores and shops, and the railway contractor Robert G. Reid was laying a track for a streetcar service through the downtown. The railway engineer R.F. Morkill goes into fine detail about how this and other services were about to be powered by the new station at Petty Harbour.

Finally, P.T. McGrath sums up life in St. John's in 1900 with an evocation of the natural features of the region and the attractions for tourists. St. John's, in his opinion, now stood as a testimony to the Anglo-Saxon spirit, and the fishing settlement of 1800 had been surpassed. "Today," he writes, "it boasts a population of thirty thousand, all of British stock, and a commerce unequalled for a town of its size." It was a bustling centre of commerce with active businessmen and hundreds of tradespeople, fishermen and laborers. The churches and schools were a credit to a city of its size, and public buildings were equally creditable, since being the seat of the colonial government, all the important departments were housed there. Newfoundland had continued to resist joining the Canadian federation, and the British system of colonial autonomy was seen in all its completeness. Moreover, the railway had disclosed a country with other sources of latent wealth: mineral belts, arable land and forests. This railway, predicts McGrath, would enable St. John's to become a tourist resort, for isolation had been removed. He is optimistic about the future since commercial and trade relations were steadily increasing. A large hotel was being built, as well as others at suitable points along the railway line.

Even though his article occasionally reads like promotion or publicity, McGrath evokes a sense of optimism and buoyancy. St. John's was moving forward, but unfortunately its progress would soon be checked by events of the twentieth century: the loss of a generation of young men during the First World War, economic depression and the failure of local government.

1

The Status Quo in 1796

"Newfoundland,"
Lloyd's Evening Post, 12-14 October 1796

The harbour of St. John's is the completest in the island of Newfoundland; its situation is in lat. 48.30 and long. 52.10. It is entirely land-locked, perfectly secure from all winds and capable of containing 300 sail of shipping. The entrance is exceedingly narrow, and, being covered by very high surrounding lands, the wind always blows directly in or out. This part is usually called the Narrows and is well defended by Fort Amherst, mounting 17 guns, and Fort Frederick, mounting nine guns; there are also two twenty-four pounders on a projection near the Chain-Rock (called Chain-Battery), admirably situate for raking an enemy coming in; but this no enemy would be rash enough to attempt unless they had first secured the new fort or Fort Townshend. This fortification has been erected since the taking of the place by the French in the last war. It is named after Lord Townshend,[5] who was Master-General of the Ordnance at the time it was erected. Being seated on an eminence, it entirely commands every part of the harbour, on which side is a battery of 22 twenty-four pounders, which it is impossible for any ship to elevate her guns high enough to incommode in the least. On the land side it is fortified as a star-fort, but not sufficiently strong to sustain an attack in a regular way. This is the residence of the Governor of the Island, who is usually a Naval Flag-Officer and who comes out in the spring and returns, before the frost sets in, for England. The garrison generally consists of two companies of regulars, one of artillery and a provincial corps of fencibles. The old fort is now in ruins and only serves for barracks for the soldiers and apartments for the military officers.

The town of St. John's is situate on the West side of the harbour. The houses are irregular and scattered. In the fishing season, which begins in May and ends in September, there are perhaps 5,000 people there; but many of them return to England annually with the ships, which in time of war rendezvous here to meet the convoy. In the harbour there are some very convenient wharfs or keys [quays] which large vessels may lie alongside of to take in their cargoes, few of the ships in this trade exceeding 300 tons burthen. The houses are built of wood and covered with shingles; should a fire happen, the consequence must be dreadful.

The adjacent country admits of very little cultivation on account of the summer being short and the winter very severe; indeed, there is very little open ground, for the country is covered with woods, which are impenetrable except by beaten paths. The plain-land is usually used for pasture, though some little grain is produced; but the crops are generally very thin. The woods are mostly composed of firs of various kinds; there is also in some parts of the Island very good timber, fit for ship-building and sometimes used as such. It is the chief and almost only employment of the inhabitants in the winter to cut wood for firing and other purposes; the smallest kind, for firing, is drawn by their large dogs, trained up and harnessed for that purpose, in which business they are tractable and useful.

In the woods are immense lakes abounding in wild fowl; but it is very difficult to get at them, except in winter. In the summer the woods are impassable, except in beaten paths; and to penetrate a few miles would take up more than double the number of hours. In the winter, when the snow is deep and frozen, it is not so difficult. There are many bears, wolves and foxes in the inland parts; but they seldom come near the settlements, except in winter. There is also plenty of game, as hares, pheasants, partridges &c., much the same as in Canada. The winter commences about the beginning of November, setting in with heavy falls of snow and severe frosts which generally last till the middle of April or beginning of May. The snowstorms are very dangerous for shipping on the coast and often attended with fatal consequences, as it is impossible to see land, though at a very small distance.

The fishing season usually begins in June and ends in September. The best and largest fish are caught on the banks, several leagues from land: for this purpose they go out in vessels 50 or 60 tons burthen and lie at anchor on the banks till they have completed their cargoes. The fish taken here are opened and salted immediately and are termed *green fish*. On account of the privateers, this mode of fishing is discontinued in time of war. At this time the fishery is carried on in shallops; these are boats of three or four tons burthen, carrying three men. They anchor near the shore in the best ground they can find, where they lie till they have filled their boats, and then return into port and, when they have unloaded, proceed again to sea for another cargo. Every man is furnished with two lines, to each of which is two hooks; one line is let down on each side, which is rarely drawn up without a fish to each hook; and the man has seldom much time to spare between baiting the hooks, hawling up the fish and baiting the hooks again: a small fish, very much resembling a smelt, called copling [capelin], is the best bait. Immense shoals of these fish visit the coasts in June and July and are taken on the beach in pailfulls; the cod often pursue these on shore to their own destruction and are taken on the beach. The flesh of penguins is often substituted as bait in lieu of copling.

The cod caught near the shore are never so large as what are taken on the banks. Those caught in this manner are gutted and the bones taken out and, after being salted, are dried in the sun on sheds made of brushwood, where they are frequently turned and the bad fish separated from the good. The best fish are shipped for Spain, Portugal and the Mediterranean, and the smallest and worst are carried to the West Indies, where it is bought up by the planters for their negroes. The fish are generally met with in sandy or gravelly bottoms but are seldom taken where it is muddy or rocky.

Bay Bulls, the first harbour which the enemy (from every information hitherto received) has taken, is situated from Cape Spear, lying S.S.E. ½ E. distant from the Narrows or entrance of St. John's harbour, four miles S.W. distant six leagues; its entrance is broad and spacious and runs up to the town of that name 1¾ mile. In working in, you carry to a regular and safe anchorage from 35 to 11 fathoms water, keeping either shore on board at a cable's length distance until you have run about 360 yards within Bread-and-Cheese Cove Point on the starboard and the keys [quays] on the larboard hand, where you may anchor from 11 to 15 fathoms water in good holding ground and ride in safety, having nothing to fear except a strong wind from S.S.E. to S.E. to which the mid-channel of the harbour lies open. Bay Bulls is distant by land from St. John's 27 miles; the path or footway leading thither is in most places so narrow, passing through the woods, small, uneven and irregular barrens (two of which lie between Bay Bulls and Petty Harbour) along the sides of stupendous hills and rocks bordering on the sea coast, and in many places the forcable parts of strong and rapid rivers running from the ponds of the interior country into the sea, that not more than a single person can with convenience pass at a time: therefore St. John's, from that quarter, may be considered tolerably secure; notwithstanding, the hostile dispositions of the

French in the year 1762 were directed from the same place and through the same channel against St. John's, which they reduced. But it should be remembered that the enemy's artillery was then landed at Quiddy Viddy, only one mile distant from the garrison of the former (a place now rendered inaccessible from the sea) and that it was then in no way competent to make such a resistance and giving such a security to the property of the inhabitants, in themselves numerous, loyal and respectable, as it is at this period, in consequence of the formidable state of the garrisons and other fortifications erected there since its recapture from the French.

Portugal Cove, situated in Conception Bay, four miles within the eastern point of Belleisle [Bell Island] and 7½ leagues W.S.W. ½ W. from Cape St. Francis, the latter bearing N. ½ E. distant seven leagues from the entrance of St. John's harbour, is a small open creek or cove, having no roadstead or shelter even for the smallest fishing craft. It lies exposed to the wind from N. by W. to N.W. by N. which heaves in a very heavy sea and obliges the few boat-keepers there to haul on their craft. It is distant from St. John's, by land, 17 miles E.S.E. ½ E.: the foot-way is well made and regular, owing to the great communications between Harbour Grace, across Conception Bay to Portugal Cove and St. John's. In the most difficult parts a man and horse may pass with ease, and these chiefly are adjacent to Portugal Cove; but the principal obstructions to the passage of a greater number extend only seven miles or thereabouts. The remaining distance to St. John's is a tolerably good road and, in all parts of its continuance to Colonel Pringle's[6] plantation (commonly called Bryant's Plantation from the present occupier) is sufficiently broad to enable men to march abreast and also convey artillery. Should it so happen that the attack is made from the southward and also at the same time from the westward, the fate of St. John's seems to be at the mercy of the enemy, for the S.W. arm of the harbour is totally unprotected, as well as the western parts of the new and old garrisons. That arm is commanded by the heights of Riverhead only half a mile from the town, which heights they pass over if they attempt to penetrate through the country from the Bay Bulls.

The French, in advancing from Portugal Cove as far as Col. Pringle's Plantation, one mile from St. John's and about three-quarters of a mile from the new garrison, may enter the town in three divisions and in three directions: first, by filing to the left on a fine open plain along Quiddy Viddy Pond about one mile and enter the town by the old garrison in an easy access to the right, about three-quarters of a mile; secondly, by advancing directly across the bridge at the head of the said pond, which lies N.N.W. half a mile from the old garrison; and thirdly, by filing to the right by Col. Pringle's Plantation, along the river about three-quarters of a mile and across the river at the side of the military road leading from the new garrison, by which means the two garrisons would be completely surrounded, except from the east, and thereby rendered totally void of any assistance from the other fortifications, which are only useful to defend the harbour from any attempt at its entrance.

2

The Start of the Nineteenth Century

Sir Robert John Pinsent (1834-1893) was born in Port de Grave and admitted to the bar in 1856. He was named to the Legislative Council in 1859. Pinsent was first elected to the Newfoundland assembly in 1867 and in 1880 was named to the Supreme Court.

Sir Robert Pinsent,
"St. John's, Newfoundland, A.D., 1800-4"
Christmas Review, 1892, 2-4

In response to the request conveyed to me by letter from the proprietors of the *Trade Review* to contribute an article to their intended Christmas number for this year of Our Lord 1892, I do not think I can do better, in this crisis of the history of St. John's, than to give an idea of its trade and condition at the commencement of this century. For this purpose I have had resort to the colonial records of the period; and, judging from my own feelings in this matter, I should think that such chronicles must be of intense interest to lovers of this country, in affording the means of making some comparison between the present and the past, in marking the progress made in the course of the century, and, perhaps, in deriving from the light of experience some guide for the future.

I need hardly say that the following pages pretend to no literary merit; they are merely the result, in describing the period with which they deal, of industrious compilation.

In the first year of this century, Admiral Pole,[7] the successor to Governor Waldegrave,[8] was Governor and Commander-in-Chief in Newfoundland, and his government included St. Pierre and Miquelon, which were now in our hands. There was still war in Europe, and the shipping of the Newfoundland trade continued to be protected by convoys; and the military and naval forces in the Island were considerable. The military forces consisted of about six hundred men under the command of Brigadier-General Skerrett.[9]

Upon the arrival of the Governor, he issued, as usual, his first Commission of the Peace, which was directed to Captains (R.N.) Ryves, Edgell and Larkan; and to civilians Jonathan Ogden, George Williams, Rev. J. Harris (St. John's); Robert Carter, Sr., Robert Carter, Jr. (Ferryland); the Rev. John Clinch, George Whittle and J. Oakley (Trinity); John Bland and Gerrard Ford (Bonavista); Charles Garland and Charles Lilly (Harbour Grace); Rev. John Dingle (Bay Bulls); J. Follett (Trepassey); J. Waldron, C.A. Cramer (Fortune Bay); John Broom (Mortier); Pierce Forristal (St. Lawrence); M. Cheater (Fogo); F. Bradshaw and J. Blackburn (Placentia). Of these, the naval captains and Messrs. Ogden, Carter, Clinch, Bland, Garland and Broom were appointed Surrogates, and Mr. Phillips continued to be High Sheriff at St. John's.

To prevent desertion, the Governor issued a proclamation announcing that a fine of £10 would be inflicted upon anyone harbouring deserters from the forces and that an equal number of the offenders' own servants would be impressed.

There seems to have been already some sort of road, with bridges, between St. John's and Ferryland, via Bay Bulls, as the Rev. Mr. Dingle, writing from Ferryland, speaks of his inability to get to Bay Bulls by reason of the heavy rains having carried away the bridges and rendered the roads impassable. He reports the death of Robert Carter, Esq., J.P., the Ferryland Surrogate. The smallpox was prevalent in St. John's and other places at this time.

By returns from the Rev. M. Harris and the Rev. Dr. O'Donnel, it appears there had been, for the past year, forty-seven baptisms, seventeen marriages and sixty-seven burials in St. John's.

The Governor received copies of H.M. Orders-in-Council, settling the royal style and title and the ensigns armorial on the union of the two kingdoms of Great Britain and Ireland.

The year 1801 appears to have been very peaceful and, in this country, very uneventful. The peace of Amiens had just been concluded.[10] The Governor was absent from the colony, and Captain Robert Burton of H.M.S. *La Concorde* administered the Government. The next year Admiral Gambier became Governor.[11] The islands of St. Pierre and Miquelon were re-delivered to the French Republic and the right of fishery held before the war restored to the French "in the manner they were entitled to enjoy the same under the Treaty of Utrecht" (Governor's Proclamation). Mr. Jonathan Ogden became Chief Justice, and Mr. George Williams succeeded him as Chief Magistrate of St. John's.

A return of the inhabitants of St. John's shews a resident population (besides the troops) of 3,420, of whom 1,139 were Protestants and 2,281 Roman Catholics. There were only five prisoners in St. John's gaol. A brewery was allowed to be erected by Mr. Haire at Mundy's Brook.

The Governor, desiring to revive the benevolent measures of Governor Waldegrave for the relief of the poor, contributed £40 towards a "charitable fund."

A system having become prevalent of harbouring, as "dieters" for the winter, persons who had arrived in the previous season for the fishery and who should, according to law, have returned to Britain, the Government issued a proclamation signifying that the houses of persons so offending would be pulled down.

A proclamation was issued against the erection, within two hundred yards from high-water mark, of anything but fishing stages and other buildings for the use of the fishery; and beyond that distance there was to be no right of private property acquired.

Certain merchants representing the hardship and inconvenience which would ensue from there not being sufficient men allowed to remain during the winter to attend to the work of building fishing rooms and boats, &c., the Governor explains that his proclamation is not intended to extend to men "duly shipped for the ensuing year."

This autumn, names of the merchants of St. John's interested in the foreign fish trade appear in a petition with regard to convoy, and it may be interesting to know who they were at the time. The signatures were as follows: Cunningham, Bell & Co., A. Thompson & Co., David Brien, McGlasher, Robertson & Co., George Gaden, R. Newman & Co., Hart & Eppes, Daniel Codner & Co., A. Hengston & Co., R. West, Bulley & Job, W. Newman & Co., Cooke and Travers, W. & R. Boden, Henry Phillips, Stuart & Rennie, G. & T. Kough, J. Hill & Co., Goss & Butler.

It appears to have been the custom at this time to farm out prisoners of war to the merchants, as a return is required of those in their employment from J. & W. Pinsent of Port-de-Grave and Gosse & Kemp of Brigus.

This, I believe, was the first country, after England, in which vaccination was introduced in place of inoculation for smallpox. A proclamation of the Governor recommends "the rendering general inoculation from the cow-pock virus" – the recent discovery of Dr. Jenner – as being of great benefit to mankind.[12] The reason that this system was so early introduced here was that the Rev. Mr. Clinch, himself a physician, was a great friend of Dr. Jenner's, and, through his advice, made very early trial of the new system in this colony.[13]

The churchyard and burial-ground were enlarged this year by exchanging, with Weston and his tenants, ground on the "Barrens" for land contiguous to the churchyard.

To show the strictness yet observed with regard to settlement, Mr. Reed, owner of the "Friendly Hall" farm, Portugal Cove Road, had to obtain permission to erect a stable and make a poultry yard.

The Governor, on leaving this year, received a highly complimentary address from the principal inhabitants. His Excellency reported to the Secretary of State that the colony was at this time prosperous and peaceable.

The principal forts, viz., Townshend, William and Amherst, were reported by Colonel Skinner[14] to be in an almost ruinous state, and that officer, besides recommending their repairs, was strong in advising the fortification of the eminence of Signal Hill and the building there of barracks, store-houses, &c.; and General Skerrett reported favourably upon the matter to the Governor for the consideration of the Master-General of the Ordnance.

The prices of provisions were at this period enormously high, and the fisheries must have been prosperous indeed to have borne them. We learn, for instance, that flour was from £2 to £3 per barrel and pork £5 to £6. The price of codfish, on the other hand, being from 14s. to 27s., according to quality, and seamen's and fishermen's wages £30 to £50 for the season.

Mr. Tremlett,[15] one of the magistrates, reported to the Governor in England, in the winter of 1803, the sudden death of the Chief Magistrate, Mr. George Williams. He also states that "the most perfect good order and regularity exist in this district and, as he is informed, in all parts of the island."

In May of 1803 the Governor was informed that the English Ambassador had left Paris and that war was again imminent, and he consequently received instructions to issue letters-of-marque[16] and commissions to privateers; and in view of this attitude of affairs, the Governor communicated with the Commander-in-

Chief of the forces at Halifax (General Bowyer), representing the necessity of strengthening the garrison at St. John's "for the defence of that place as well from any attack of the enemy as from the seditious disposition of some of the lower classes of the inhabitants" until a regiment should have been raised in Newfoundland.

About this time the Crown officers give their opinion that the English Poor Laws did not apply to this island and that the Governor has no power to enforce payment of rates towards building or repairing churches.

Mr. Tremlett was appointed Chief Justice in place of Mr. Ogden, who had resigned from ill-health. The Chief Justice, with the High Sheriff and other officers, was conveyed on circuit by H.M.S. *Falcon*, Captain Ommaney.

A native Indian woman, captured by William Cull,[17] was brought to St. John's. He had undertaken that she should return to her friends with articles of clothing, &c. Cull received a reward of £50 for this service in the cause of intercourse and conciliation with the native tribes.

Arrangements were made by the Governor for the making of a carriage road through the plantation called "the Forest," on the south side of Quidi Vidi Lake. This was opposed by some persons, such as are ever to be found resenting improvement, upon the ground that the wood-path was sufficient and that the wood might suffer. The Governor, with the inhabitants generally, persevered, and thus became established the road known to this day as the "Forest Road."

Mr. Thomas Coote was appointed Chief Magistrate, *vice* Williams, deceased.

Many vessels in the trade were at this, as at other times of warfare, commissioned by letters of marque as armed ships. The famous firm of Spurrier & Joliffe had no less than fourteen ships thus commissioned at one time, and I notice, amongst others, the

Highland Lass, belonging to Messrs. Hunters & Co. (a St. John's firm existing in very recent times), of 554 tons burthen, mounting 16 six-pounders and carrying thirty-five officers and men; also the ship *William*, Hill master, owned by John and William Pinsent of London (and Port-de-Grave), merchants, of the burthen of 283 tons, mounting twelve connonades (twelve pounders) and navigated by twenty-five men.

I do not think I have before mentioned that former Chief Justice, Mr. [Richard] Routh, had left this country on leave of absence on a voyage to England in the autumn of 1800 but had never since been heard of. His widow was this year allowed to receive the salary which had accrued since then until the appointment of Mr. Routh's successor in 1802, and a pension was conferred upon her.

In 1804, Admiral Sir Erasmus Gower[18] became Governor. Soon after his arrival the principal inhabitants of St. John's memorialized him for his influence in favour of a provision for "the Right Rev. James O'Donnel,[19] chief Roman Catholic clergyman of this island," who, they say, "has resided among us for twenty years, during which time he has strenuously and successfully labored to improve the morals and regulate the conduct of the planters, tenants and lower classes." They speak of the extensive influence he had acquired over the lower classes, by which means they were prevented from joining the mutineers of the Newfoundland regiment at a time when General Skerrett had not sufficient force to oppose such a dangerous combination; and the memorialists concluded by earnestly requesting His Excellency to use his "benevolent influence with H.M. Ministers to reward this very respectable gentleman some little independence during the short remainder of a long life spent in the service of his King, country and neighbours." The Governor replied that it would give him great pleasure to attend to this request. The result of this application was an annuity of £50 stg. to the good Bishop, who in writing to the Governor expressing his great gratitude to him and the gentlemen who had memorialized the Crown on the subject, remarks that they "over-rated my slender endeavours to promote loyalty, peace and good-will among His Majesty's subjects here, which I always deemed a duty strictly incumbent upon me; and while I have a tongue to speak or a head to think, I will not desist from pursuing the same line of conduct which I have done those twenty-one years"; and Dr. O'Donnel concludes with the expression of "great veneration and cordial esteem" for His Excellency.

The surrogates and magistrates were directed by the Governor that, unless the merchants made known to the planters and boat-keepers by the first of August the prices of goods and of fish and oil, they were, in the event of litigation, to allow only the lowest prices charged for goods and the highest for fish and oil.

The Board of Ordnance allowed £2,530 towards the erection of barracks and other military works at Signal Hill.

Notwithstanding the Act of X. and XI. William 3, cap. 35, the character of the town as a strict fishing settlement only was rapidly changing, as is evidenced by a proclamation reciting that the harbour of St. John's was greatly injured as a fishing station by the number of dwelling houses, retail shops, public houses and gardens crowded together in the lower part of the town where flakes formerly stood and where it was to be hoped that, as the fishery recovered its former activity and extent, they will be again required. It is declared that His Majesty's instruction as to the erections to be made within two hundred yards from high-water mark confine these to such as are built for the express purpose of the fishery.

The changing nature of the trade of St. John's and of the island and the greatly modified conditions under which business was now being carried on is shewn in a report from the Chief Justice, Sheriff and Magistrates to the Governor in August 1804.

The "Society for Improving the Conditions of the Poor" obtained a site for a schoolhouse, which would appear to be that afterwards, and until the recent fire, taken up by the Newfoundland (now the Colonial and Continental) School Society and the "Old Factory."

We learn this year (1804) for the first time of any project for making a regular street outside Water Street; but now for the purpose of providing accommodation for artificers, shopkeepers and others not connected with the fishery and who now intruded upon the space set apart for the fisheries, the Governor (Gower) caused a road to be marked out, thirty feet wide, between the distance of 200 and 210 yards from high-water mark, with permission to persons to build on the upper side of this road, facing the harbour, they, in return for this permission, paying from £5 to £10 into the fund for the relief of the poor. This was the road afterwards named and now known as Gower Street.

The Phœnix Fire Company presented the town of St. John's with a fire engine, and the British and Imperial Companies presented thirty-five fire buckets.

There was a project in view for the erection of a "Town House and Market Place" to be built below the churchyard; but it appears this design fell through.

The fishery for this year is reported as being very successful; the number of adventurers and passengers from the old country had diminished; the recruiting of the Newfoundland regiment had met with great success; a woman was hanged for the murder of her husband and a clerk in the navy sentenced to death (commuted to transportation for life) for forgery. The Poor School had been erected and an industrial department established in connection with it capable of admitting 400 children. Leases of land near St. John's for cultivation, to the extent of about 300 acres, had been granted this year. The increasing importance of the seal fishery, "yet in its infancy," is shewn in the fact that 100 sail of vessels with 1,200 men had been employed in it during the past season. The Bank fishery, prosecuted by adventurers from Great Britain, which in 1788 was represented by 330 ships, now employed only thirty. The fishery had become almost wholly sedentary. The export trade of the island was valued at about £700,000 to £800,000, of which nearly half went from St. John's, now become the chief emporium of the trade of the island. The entire permanent population of Newfoundland was at this time about 25,000 and that of St. John's itself under 4,000. With such a trade for so limited a population, it may be imagined that just at this time the colony was in a high state of prosperity. Rapid fortunes were being made and carried away; but the industrial classes, while they shared for a time in the common abundance, were enabled to lay up little or nothing for themselves for the "rainy day."

3

The First Millionaire

The Most Rev. Michael Francis Howley (1843-1914) was the son of a prosperous St. John's merchant who had emigrated from Ireland in the early nineteenth century. Ordained to the priesthood in 1868, he was Prefect Apostolic of St. George's, 1886-92; Bishop of St. John's, 1894-1904; and Archbishop of St. John's, 1904-1914.

Most Rev. Michael Francis Howley,
**"How Meagher Became a Millionaire:
A True Story of Old St. John's"**
Newfoundland Quarterly, 4 (3), (1904): 2-3

The splendid harbour facilities of St. John's, its easy access from the Atlantic, the aptitude of the surrounding land for the site of a town and the suitableness of its surrounding valleys for an agricultural settlement rendered it from the beginning a most likely place for the founding of the capital city of the Colony. Hence although Ferryland and Placentia had the advantage of it in priority of selection and in the expenditure of vast sums of money in the erection of military works, &c., yet these places, not having the natural advantages of St. John's, yielded to it in the course of time, and about the beginning of the XVIII century we find St. John's the acknowledged capital and the residence of the Governor.

It was not, however, until the early decades of the XIX century that she began to "change her character from a fishery to a large commercial town" (Governor Keats's[20] letter to Lord Bathurst in Prowse, p. 399).[21] The population of the city at that time was 10,000, and immigrants were constantly pouring in, principally from Ireland. Between the years 1814 and 1815 as many as eleven thousand immigrants came from Ireland. Kent & Morris had a regular passenger service by sailing vessels from Waterford. Newfoundland was blessed in those days with two enlightened and broad-minded governors, viz.: Admiral Sir John T. Duckworth, who came in 1810, and Admiral Sir Richard Goodwin Keats, who succeeded him in 1812.

Under these progressive men, great improvements were made in St. John's and its environs. The "Ships' Fishing Rooms," which had monopolized the best sites in the town, were abolished. The laws forbidding the erection of permanent houses were repealed; grants of land were made in small lots in the suburbs (the grant of "Mount Cashel" lands date back to this period, 1815); more than a thousand acres of land were then under cultivation. The streets of the city were laid out on an improved and enlarged plan; a police force was established, also a fire brigade, and an attempt was made at lighting and sewerage.

In the year 1812 the second American war broke out, and it was a harvest time for the merchants of St. John's. Many a "fortune" was made in those years, and of one of these I am going to tell the story. Judge Prowse in his admirable history gives a graphic sketch of St. John's in these days (p. 387 et seq.): "During the whole conflict (the American war) Newfoundland was in a state of great prosperity, wages were high . . . fish and oil and all our produce was also abnormally high." St. John's was the base of operations of the British fleet during the war. "There were in the harbour at the breaking out of the war three sail of the line, twenty-one frigates and thirty-seven sloops, brigs and schooners of war." Prizes were constantly being brought in laden with various cargoes, many of them of very great value. At one time there were thirty American prizes in the harbour. "I have heard a gentleman describe his walking across from Bennett's (now Duder's) to Alsop's on the Southside on American prizes chained together... On board the captured vessels were all sorts of valuable freights – Lyons silks and whole cargoes of champagne &c." (Prowse, p. 387).

Among the mercantile houses of St. John's about the year 1815 was that of Meagher & Sons. Their premises were situated about where Tessier's are now. On an old code of signals in my possession (for which I am indebted to our local artist Jno. Hayward, Esq.),[22] I find Meagher's house flag. It is all green with a large yellow capital M in the centre. He was a very wealthy merchant, owning several foreign-going vessels. He, like many others, having amassed a large fortune, returned to live in his native country. Before proceeding to tell how he started on his career of success, I must say a few words concerning the family history of the head of this firm.

Among the Irish immigrants who came to Newfoundland about this time was a young man, a native of Clonmel, named Thomas Meagher. He was a tailor by trade and worked at first in the establishment of Mr. Crotty, a man who carried on a large tailoring and clothing business. Young Meagher was a shrewd businessman and a great favourite in the household. Mr. Crotty died, and in due course of time Meagher married the widow and became owner of the whole business. There was a romance connected with this Crotty which it would be out of place to relate here but which may form the subject of a future Christmas story.

During this stirring period scarcely a day passed on which there was not a sale of goods from the cargoes of the prizes brought into the harbour by the British men-o'-war.

One day a prize was brought laden with delf[23] [*sic*] crockeryware and glassware packed in crates. A sale was called by the town crier. Mr. Meagher, who besides his clothing business always had an eye to "the main chance," was punctually on the ground at all these sales. Seeing that the goods in this case were not of much value, he agreed with William Thomas, another prominent merchant of those times, to go "halves" for one crate "just to keep their hands in." The crate was knocked down to Mr. Meagher "for a mere song," and the auctioneer, seeing that there was going to be no bidding that day, was about to close down the sale when a commotion was heard on the outskirts of the crowd. The Commissary or Quartermaster of the military at the time was a certain Captain Barnes. He was a jovial and convivial character and was well known through the town as a perpetrator of innumerable practical jokes and the performance of many bold and daredevil feats. He was seen riding along the street until he reached the scene of the auction when he reined in his horse. It was evident from his rollicking manner and the somewhat unsteady way in which he sat his horse that he was returning from some carousal and was not quite himself.

Flourishing his whip he forced his way through the crowd, cracking jokes right and left. On learning that the sale was about to be called off, "Come, Mr. -------," he cried, "I'll take the whole d---- lot of them! I want the crates to make coops for my spring chickens. You may pitch the cups and saucers over the wharf, but send up the crates to the Ordnance Yard at once." He went off whistling a lively air and thinking no more about the matter. The auctioneer knocked down the whole lot, some couple of dozen, to the Captain and prepared to have them carted to his residence.

In the meantime, it having been agreed between Meagher and Thomas that he (Meagher) should take the crate home and unpack it and send half the contents back to him (Thomas), Meagher had the crate carted to his house and placed in the back workroom. He waited till night-time, when his journeymen had all gone home, before commencing to unpack.

No sooner had he removed the first tier of delf-ware than he stood amazed and astonished, for there before his eyes he saw the rarest selection of valuable silks with which the whole interior of the crate was closely packed! He could scarcely draw his breath, so excited was he as he took out one after another rolls and packages of the most brilliant and costly fabrics: silk stuffs woofed with wool and with gold and silver threads forming the most exquisite patterns; shawls, handkerchiefs scarves, watered silks, poplins, velvets, satinets, moires &c. – it was simply bewildering. It had been the intention, of course, to introduce these articles as contraband to America.

Mr. Meagher quietly packed all the goods into trunks, safely locked them and carefully concealed them. The delf-ware, of which there was only an outer layer all round the crate buried in straw, he religiously divided and in the morning sent one half over to Mr. Thomas but said not a word about the silks. Thomas made some slight remark about the smallness of the quantity but was easily led to believe that the greater part of the ware had been broken.

When Commissary Barnes awoke next morning, having slept off his debauch, he was surprised to hear a great noise and commotion going on outside. Looking out of his window he saw the square of the Ordnance Yard encumbered with the immense crates and horses and carts still bringing more. He could not understand what it was all about. He had quite forgotten his freak of the day before. In the course of the day, however, his memory began to clear up, and it was helped by a sharp reprimand from the commanding officer of the garrison, who had come to learn of the absurd purchase. He was reminded that his position debarred him from entering into commercial enterprises, and he was ordered to send back at once the ridiculous articles or to pay from his own pocket the amount of the bill. The auctioneer, of course, would not hear of taking back the articles, and the consternation of poor Barnes, whose salary was not over large, was quite pitiable, besides his confusion at being made the laughing stock of the whole garrison.

While in this miserable plight, Mr. Meagher came like a good angel to his relief, happening along, as it were, by mere chance and with an air of complete innocence. He got into conversation with Barnes, sympathized deeply with him in his distress and finally, in a burst of most magnanimous generosity, he said, "I'll tell you what, Barnes. Without any inconvenience to myself, I can help you out of this difficulty. In my shop I do a little of all kinds of business, so I'll take the crates off your hands. Of course, I know I may have to wait a long time to realize them, as there is an overstock of crockeryware in town just now. But I have compassion for you; you're not a bad fellow, and I like to help a poor devil out of a mess."

"My dear fellow," shouted Barnes, squeezing him by the hand, "I'll never forget this noble act! To tell the truth, it saves me from court marshal and degradation, for I assure you I'm deucedly hard up, and I never could find the money to pay for those crates! I thank you most sincerely."

Meagher lost no time in getting the crates home and settling the auctioneer's account. For weeks after, he spent his nights locked up in his workroom assorting and packing into trunks and portmanteaux the contents of the crates. All were filled with valuable goods like the first one.

That fall, Meagher went home. The number of trunks and portmanteaux he brought with him excited some comment, but he said it was ready-mades that he was supplying to the Irish trade. When he returned in the spring, he brought out a whole cargo of goods for the general trade of the Island and seemed also to have an unlimited supply of money. He bought a waterside premises, as mentioned above. He soon became one of our wealthiest merchants. After a few years, having amassed a large fortune, he retired to Ireland and spent his last days in Waterford.

He had two sons, Patrick and Thomas. Patrick became a priest and a Jesuit and was the first Newfoundlander promoted to Holy Orders. Thomas, who was also born in Newfoundland, was the father of Thomas F. Meagher, the famous "Young Irelander" – the Vergniaud[24] of the rising of '48.[25]

4

Reminiscences of Elias Durnford

Henry W. LeMessurier (1848-1931) was born and educated in St. John's and spent 60 years as a civil servant. From 1889, he edited the *Evening Herald*. LeMessurier also influenced the introduction of curling in Newfoundland and is remembered for his song "The Ryans and the Pittmans."

H.W. LeMessurier, **"Reminiscences of Old St. John's"**
Newfoundland Quarterly, 10 (3), 1916

The town of St. John's in 1800 was a garrison town, and the troops required for service therein were principally drafted from England. Prior to 1800, part of a regiment of Highlanders was stationed here and occupied the barracks at Signal Hill. Owing to the coldness of the winter, the men were ordered to wear "breeks," which were served out to them from the military stores. This order almost raised a mutiny among them; the commanding officer, however, managed to persuade them to obey the order, but when they came to town on leave, they often took off the "breeks" and carried them over their arms.

The getting to Newfoundland from Europe in those days was a tedious business. Sailing ships were the only means of conveyance, and oftentimes these had to be convoyed by vessels of the Navy. Miss Durnford, in *Family Recollections*,[26] tells of the coming of her father, Lt.-Gen. E. Durnford, R.E., and his family to this country in 1809. He embarked at Portsmouth in the Britannia transport in the summer and left in company with a large fleet of merchant vessels and transports for America. A line of battleships conveyed the Commodore with Sir George Provost, the newly appointed Governor of Canada, and several frigates accompanied the fleet. The flag-ship carried 64 guns.

"Each phase of momentous time's revolvement offers its peculiarities of development; nor can the floating assemblage of life, collected on the occasion of a favourable convoy, be considered without interest when launched together on the uncertain ocean and offering to each other in nautical companionship a partial diversion from the usual monotony of sea voyages. Some degree of discipline and attention was necessarily maintained; all must obey the signalized orders of the protecting ship whenever the speaking pennant fluttered from the masthead. Sometimes a presumptuous sail was warned from aspiring to be foremost by a heavy gun being fired; now some light bark was ordered to take in tow a slow sailing vessel, or at the different longitudes the variously bound ships were told when to part company. The *Britannia*, being a heavily laden brig and sometimes in the rear of the fleet, was consequently several times helped on by the swift sailing frigate *Le Bon Citoyen's* towing cable. Once while thus agreeably propelled, a sudden squall snapped the rope, not without danger to the cast-off brig. *Le Bon Citoyen* afterwards departed [the] convoy to go in chase of a suspicious-looking sail."

Every occurrence at sea, however trivial, is stamped with importance. The appearance of a whale, the gambolling of porpoises, a sight of the ominous seabird "Mother Carey's Chickens," looked on as sure forerunners of the storm, a barrel or cork floating on the wave, above all a strange sail on the horizon, rivet eager observation and curiosity. Delightful was the chance when one fine morning's tantalizing calm enabled the transfer of a bottle of milk from the *Britannia* to the friendly master of another vessel; the neck of the bottle was inserted in a rope and floated from one ship to the other, milk being supplied by General Durnford's cow. Mr. Cummins, the master of the Britannia, was fond of talking of the complaints made against his brothers in the trade by officers consigned to their treatment. These he confessed were often just; but he laughed much at one grievance: a party of gentlemen alleged as among the annoying vexations of their uncomfortable voyage being served with none but broken biscuits. He maintained that only the best biscuits broke. When the Great Bank was reached, the *Britannia* hove to for several hours to allow the ship's crew the pleasure of fishing, and truly wonderful was the draft of fish. The lines were thrown in and drawn up without a moment's intermediate delay, sometimes two large cod coming up on the same hook. Again setting sail, they were soon greeted by a fragrant land smell, announcing proximity to Newfoundland, and the abrupt features of its wild, fir-clad shores came to view.

Newfoundland was at that time only known to the world by virtue of the fame of its celebrated fishing Banks, one of the first discoveries made in the New World by the Cabots. Neglect reposed over the cultivation of the soil, while the rocks of Newfoundland had become proverbial; and the very infant playing under its flakes threatened to "heave a rock" at his fellow ragamuffin. It may not be out of place to relate how it had obtained this character in Europe, among the refined of courts and the cultivated in senate. The rough British adventurers engaged in the fisheries were, in 1762, surprised by the French, who, in that year, invaded and easily took possession of the Island. Immediately the news reached General Amherst, on his own responsibility and without waiting for orders from Home, he detached his brother with a body of forces here. These speedily recovered the Island, regained all that had been taken and made the French commander prisoner. The right of the French for their loss was brought forward by Mr. Fox in one of his eloquent speeches: the Duc de Choiseul, he said, "asked for but one rock at Newfoundland." His humble request was, "Donnez-nous un rocher seulement." This humble request was granted. But, alas! What they asked for their bâtiments-pêcheurs extended to much more than a rock. There was succeeding encroachment and attendant vexation.

A few days after arriving in St. John's, Capt. Ross, R.E., the officer whom General Durnford relieved, sailed from it in full elation of spirit at the prospect of soon seeing Portugal and sharing in glory's sublunary reward. Not many weeks afterwards, this generous young man sent presents to the friends he had quitted of the fine fruits the golden country he had reached yielded. A few days following, these friends received intelligence his head had been shot off at the siege of Sebastian.[30]

"In the rock-girt Island of Newfoundland, fertile wherever its soil has been subjected to cultivation and whose atmosphere's dense fogs seem to drop down revivification and nourishment among the swarming myriads its vast Banks teem with, General Durnford remained until 1816. England, sensible of the value of this evergreen land, has always guarded it by a strong naval force and at that time entrusted the direction of its affairs to an admiral, the period of whose government was limited to three consecutive summer visits. The fir-covered heights overlooking the entrance to the harbor of the chief town, St. John's, is planted with batteries romantically situated. The raging surf of the Atlantic's billows dashes against the embrasures of Amherst and Chain Rock Batteries: lobsters of the finest flavour and other shellfish are found in abundance amid the crevices of their shelving and slippery rocks with hosts of mollusca; and the line of battleships, as well as the red-sailed fishing skiffs, come almost within arm's reach of the cannon. Midway, and crowning the eminence, guns commandingly point from the Queen's Battery, Frederick's Battery and the lines on Signal Hill; and other defensive positions are placed among wooded projections of capes and bays, fragrant with spruce, juniper &c.

Generally, wherever the ground was laid open by clearance, the kalmia sprang up, an indigenous shrub or weed, brightening the wilderness with its pink clusters. Fantastic and delicate creepers present a trellised carpet to the foot that treads within the sombre shade of the woods; and varieties of graceful shrubs produce spontaneously the cranberry or oxycoccus, whose Indian name is Maskigo Meino; the whortleberry or vaccinium; the partridge or mitchella, whose tiny wreath almost vies in beauty with that of the famed capillaire or linnae, yet without the fragrance of the last; and the hardy little dogwood or cornus. There is much to admire in the decorations of its hills and valleys, its ferns and intricacies of wreathing foliage, clinging to and twining round tapering firs and valuable spruce trees. The beautiful white moss crushes beneath the feet, and another species hangs in tufts among the branches of the fir forests.

Newfoundland's steep and abrupt shores, covered from the water's edge in most parts with evergreen wood and often enveloped in fog, have ever been a terror to mariners when, by chance misreckoning or adverse gales driven upon the treacherous rocks and perils, many of its headlands present when concealed by thick mist. Fearful and frequent at that time were shipwrecks on the coast."

In the American War of 1812, Newfoundland cruelly suffered. The commercial intercourse with the harbour of St. John's was obstructed in 1812, while destitute of the protection of any ship of war, by the appearance of an American armed vessel very near the entrance. This alarmed the merchants, who immediately applied to General Moore for the aid of fifty volunteers from the troops in garrison, who decided that each corps would furnish a proportionate quota. Two corporals and six privates of sappers cheerfully joined the other detachments and embarked in a brig fitted out by the merchants. As soon as the American saw the movement of the British vessel, it took its departure and was not seen again.

Deep snow and high drifts debarred, during the long winter months, all field exercises to the troops, though fearful at this season were the risks to which the soldiers on duty, visiting officers and relieving parties were exposed. The sentinel was not infrequently found frozen to death, and while the tempest of a *poudrée* was battling, life was often hazarded in visiting by night the various detached posts. While the intense frost hung into icicles the breath from the nostrils and lips and nipped with the pang of extreme cold the extremities of the human body, the strict discipline of war was maintained at St. John's and no relaxation of its severity permitted. General Durnford took his regular turn in the garrison duty, first as captain, latterly as field officer. He took pleasure in the regularity and exact observance of morning parades, and whilst performing the services of aide-de-camp prided himself in mounting on these occasions an old charger of the Duke of Kent,[31] a faithful bay that in memory of by-gone distinction always persisted in stepping foremost of the general's staff. This horse was purchased in Halifax when the Duke of Kent surrendered his command of that station and was subsequently brought to Newfoundland.

Miss Durnford's reminiscences are very interesting and give us an idea of life in the Colony at that period. I may at a later date be able to furnish my readers with more notes from her *Recollections*.

5

The State of Society in 1815

"A Hundred Years Ago"

Colonial Commerce, 25 (1), (1915): 25-27

There are usually some valuable lessons to be learned by comparing the age that we live in with bygone days. We propose to take a retrospect of the trade and commerce of the Colony a hundred years ago. Waterloo had been fought and Napoleon had abdicated and was getting his first experience of the lonely isolation of St. Helena. The second treaty of Paris between England and France involving the Newfoundland fishery question had been ratified, confirming the Treaty of Versailles in 1783. The price of fish went down in the foreign markets and caused a lot of failures both in Newfoundland and amongst the bankers and business people of England with whom the St. John's and outport merchants had dealings. Many a Newfoundland planter was hopelessly ruined by leaving his money on the books. Captain Buchan, R.N.,[32] took possession of St. Pierre and Miquelon on the 26th of August.

The previous year, 1814, 1,200,000 quintals of fish had been exported and good prices were realized. In 1815, the imports were worth £659,280 and the exports £1,183,800. The number of quintals of codfish exported in 1815 was 1,247,503, tons of oil 7,632, sealskins 126,315. The number of ships [that] entered

St. John's and outports with foreign cargoes was 874. The number cleared was about 900.

A census of the people of St. John's was taken by Lionel Chancey[33] in the summer of 1815 which showed that there were 10,018 people in the city. Of these, 2,465 were boarders, all men except 197. The number of Catholics was 7,532 and Protestants 2,486. The District Divisions in the Census List were: (1) From River Head to Pages Corner; (2) From Page's Corner to Burst-Heart Hill; (3) From Burst-Heart Hill to Church Hill; (4) From Church Hill to Hunter's Cove; (5) From Hunter's Cove to King's Wharf; (6) From King's Wharf to Fort William; (7) From Fort William to Quidi Vidi. The South Side was a District Division and contained 197 people. In Torbay, Portugal Cove, Petty Harbour, Pouch Cove and Bell Island there were only 1,856 people.

There were 23,000 seals taken the previous spring by St. John's crews and 61,000 in all Conception Bay, where 68 vessels sailed to the ice with 1,227 men. There were five vessels out of Trinity with 76 men who brought in 8,538 seals. In Ferryland, 4,700 seals were taken, and 20,108 were landed in Bonavista Bay, mostly hauled by landsmen. The salmon fishery was a great industry in those days, and the price went as high as 80 shillings a tierce [cask].

In 1815, after the most strenuous opposition on the part of the business people to the idea of taxation of sixpence a gallon, £11,888 was collected in duty on rum. To read the arguments set up by the citizens of St. John's of this day against the intention of putting a tax of sixpence a gallon on rum, one will find a fund of piquant amusement and food for reflection. £10,349 was collected on rum from the West Indies and £1,539 on the same article from other countries. The total duty, including a few hundred pounds on molasses and coffee, amounted to £16,954. There was also a small duty on sugar. Petitions were sent to the

Home Government when it was proposed to tax rum sixpence a gallon, saying that the trade of Newfoundland would be ruined and the people would not be able to stand it.

The salaries paid to the public officials, £5,080. The Governor received £800; Chief Justice £1,000; seven surrogate judges £60 each, but they had a good many sidelines and were never in want of a bag or a barrel. The Judge of the Admiralty was paid £500, while the Clerk of the Supreme Court had to be satisfied with £70. The Sheriff evidently had a pull or may be that he was called upon to hang so many people during his term of office that £252 was considered a fair salary for him.

In the summer of 1814 and 1815, no less than 11,000 Irishmen came to St. John's. Many went out to Prince Edward Island in the fall after one summer at the fishery, and also a good percentage went in American traders to the United States. There was too much fish caught in 1815 to have a good price. From 40 shillings the previous season it dropped 19 shillings. When the year closed there came a crash. As many as 700 writs were issued in November, and forty houses, big and small, had to declare insolvent.

The importation of provisions fell off on the closing up of so many houses, and in the winter great destitution set in. The Benevolent Irish Society[34] did great service in relieving the destitute Irishmen. James McBraire was President, and he gave also generously out of his private fortune to relieve the distress. No creed and no nationality was refused assistance. Only for this organized aid, many would, no doubt, have died of starvation. Scores of big business men in the outports went to the wall. It was a terrible winter in St. John's. We, living a hundred years after, can have no adequate idea of the state of society then prevailing.

Let us consider a few of the conveniences of civilized life that we have and they had to do without. They had no steam service, no railways, no telegraphs – a primitive mail service started seven years before, where the posting of a letter cost a shilling to two and six – no envelopes, no electric light, not even gas, nor yet kerosene oil. Cod oil lamps were used by the poor and candles by the well-to-do. Most people "dipped" their own candles. No friction matches, the flint-and-steel were the prime and principal source of their fires, but most people kept live coals in a heap of ashes under an upturned pot over night. The men lit their pipes with a live coal, or what was usually termed a "bran." There were no stoves – all had open fireplaces – or, in the case of merchants, ranges with a Dutch oven on the side. The only coal used was brought from Newcastle, England, in the merchants' ships. Only the rich could afford to buy it.

Nine-tenths of the residents, in the words of the old song, "went in the woods with their dogs and tackelins" and cut their spruce, fir and birch from eight to twelve inches in the butt in the vicinity of Long Pond, Mundy's Pond and a mile north of Military Road. The man who went in beyond Nagle's Hill or the present site of the Ropewalk was regarded as a hero of the Nansen[35] type, and all his friends and neighbours crowded into his house in the night to hear of his wonderful trip while sitting in front of the big blazing fire that eat up his whole day's work in a few hours. The people living east of Burst Heart Hill [now Carter's Hill] used to cut their winter's wood along Forest Road, where the Llewellyn Grounds and the cemeteries are today, and both sides of Quidi Vidi Lake were well wooded with fir and birch. Forest Road retains this today, the name given to it in the first years of the nineteenth century. A picture of Water Street in those days would be worth its weight in gold to the native antiquarian. Most of the houses were of wood, and the street was so narrow down about the present Seamen's Institute [King George V Institute] that people could almost touch hands from the windows upstairs. In the East and West Ends – from

Hutchings Street up and from King's Wharf down to the extreme end of Maggotty Cove – the street was covered with flakes.

As one walked along to go to Signal Hill, what fell through the flake boughs and longueurs onto the head and shoulders of the pedestrians gave rise to the name Maggotty Cove. It is true that there were a good many large and improving structures along the waterfront – merchants' stores for dry goods and provisions, stores for fish and oil – both seal and cod oil. When the big fire came a few years after, it is easy to imagine how quickly the whole of Water Street was laid in ashes. Military Road was a mere footpath used by the soldiers going from Fort William to Fort Townshend. On the site where the R.C. Cathedral stands, the military at the latter fort had their wood yard, and one of the principal arguments put up against Bishop Fleming when he was struggling to get a grant of land was that "the military would have no place to stock their wood."

As to the other inventions of civilization, there were no sewing machines, no banks and only one newspaper, which was presented specially for the Governor and a few officials – the *Royal Gazette.* The phonograph, telephone, automobile, submarine ands aeroplane were only hinted of in dreams on the pages of the *Arabian Nights*. The town did not extend northerly beyond New Gower Street in the east and beyond the ridge of Carter's Hill and Barter's Hill in the west. Looking back at the primitive state of society in St. John's in 1815 and the ever-threatening and intermittent spells of hard and hungry times, we today ought to feel thankful to Divine Providence that we are living in the midst of plenty and that our cod fishery is no greater than it was then, that we are enjoying all the blessings and requirements of a happy community.

6

The Fire of 1817

"Another Calamitous Fire at St. John's. Newfoundland"
Aberdeen Chronicle, 20 December 1817, 2-3
[from the *Mercantile Journal*, 21 November]

About half-past three o'clock this morning, just as we were about to put our paper to press, we were alarmed by a signal of fire; and we have now the painful task to record, after so short a lapse of time, another extensive and distressing conflagration.

It appears that the fire was observed in the premises of Messrs. Huie, Reid and Co. in Water Street and soon extended its ravages to the westward as far as the house of Mr. Benjamin Bowering, on the upper side, and the store of Mr. Robt. Nevins, on the lower, where by very powerful exertions it was stopped in its westerly direction but continued advancing eastward until about half-past nine o'clock, by which time it had burnt the premises of Mr. James Clift, where great exertions were required and were happily exerted to save the premises of Messrs. Perkins and Winter, upon which depended the safety of the whole range of houses on the Church Hill, on the upper side, and the stores of Messrs. Trimminghams and Co. on the lower side, just where the late fire was stopped in its progress westward, all of which narrowly escaped on the 7th inst. Thus a great part of the western half of the town, which we contemplated as a shelter for the then distressed, is laid in ashes, and many families have to lament and feel the painful distress of a second time being burnt out of their dwellings in the short space of fourteen days – by what means many of them will find shelter the approaching winter, we are at a loss to conjecture, should they even be fortunate enough to have the means of purchasing necessaries.

In this hasty account we cannot enter fully into the particulars, nor can we at this short notice pretend to estimate the aggregate amount of the damage done; the very extensive stores and dwellings of Messrs. Cunningham, Bell and Co. and those of Messrs, Huie, Reid and Co., Ryan and Sons, Mr. Robert Nivens, Mr. James Clift, Mr. John Burke and several other mercantile establishments have fallen a sacrifice to the devouring flames; the dwelling-house, shop &c. of Mr. Nivens were preserved.

Too much praise cannot be bestowed on the navy, military and an immense number of the respectable inhabitants for their united exertions in stopping the fire, whose efforts were directed and supported by the civil authorities and the clergy, particularly the Rev. Father Fitzgerald;[36] and although we could mention numerous other individuals highly deserving, yet in justice to his merit we are constrained to notice him particularly.

Various conjectures are afloat as to the cause of this disaster, but we will not at present hazard an opinion. We have great confidence that the proclamations of His Excellency the Governor and the decisive measures adopted by the civil authorities relative to depredations committed on the property of sufferers in the late fire will have the effect of preventing, in a great degree, similar atrocities on the present occasion:

St. John's, Nov. 24

"We have now to state that in addition to this calamitous fire of the 7th inst. we have experienced another dreadful conflagration on the 21st, which in a few hours consumed 55 houses (in addition to the 135 formerly destroyed) besides stores and wharfs of many respectable mercantile establishments. At one time we apprehended we should have betaken ourselves to the woods, for the fire would certainly have destroyed all the remaining western part of the town, had it not fortunately been a calm at the time it broke out, which enabled the inhabitants to stop its progress westward. The plunder committed is most dreadful and extensive.

"Captain Riddle was again conspicuous in arresting the progress of the flames. His enterprise and services deserve the thanks of the community; the police and the clergy are also very active; by the exertions of the two latter, great part of the stolen property is daily restored.

"List of merchants whose stores were destroyed by fire at Newfoundland, 21st November 1817: Murphy and Gleeson; Robert Nevins; Huie, Reid and Co.; Anthony Godfrey; Cunningham, Bell and Co.; Ryan and Sons; (lower stores); Dan Ryan; James Clift."

7

How Criminals Used to be Punished Severely

Henry Francis Shortis (1855-1935), born in Harbour Grace, began his career as a telegrapher in Harbour Grace and Heart's Content. He then became a journalist in St. John's and later postmaster for the Newfoundland railway. Shortis was also a founding member of the Newfoundland Historical Society in 1905.

H.F. Shortis,
"How Criminals Were Punished in the Old Days"
Papers of H.F. Shortis
Provincial Archives of Newfoundland and Labrador, vol.7, 84

From the most authentic sources, I have garnered my compilation, and I am sure it will interest my readers. It must be understood that in the days in which these punishments were imposed, surrogate courts existed. The late Judge Pinsent[37] of the Supreme Court said in one of his articles, "With the defiant progress of settlement and the changing and advancing spirit and requirements of the age, the Surrogate Courts were found to be inconsistent and intolerable." The famous Butler and Lundrigan cases, in which men of these names were flogged for contempt of court at the stage head, led in 1824 to the Act of Parliament abolishing the surrogate courts and the establishment of the Supreme Court as it is now constituted.

In my perusal of some old records, I notice that a deposition was made by a man residing at Bonavista in the year 1749 in relation to a robbery having been committed – a pair of women's shoes and buckles which had never been worn and which had cost him seven shillings and sixpence sterling. He examined many persons until he at last found the shoes in the possession of a woman – he saw the buckles of a later date in possession of a man who was wearing them in his shoes. The man and woman were brought before court. The man, who was proven to be the culprit, the woman having purchased the shoes with the understanding that they were procured in an honest manner, was ordered to receive fifteen strips on the bare back by the hands of the Beadle at the public whipping post. The magistrate said, "Having some hints that a mob would gather upon the occasion, I went myself to see it executed but was hindered near an hour by arguments on behalf of the culprit, chiefly by his master, who said he wanted to have another hearing about it, but at length, having got to the culprit at the post, before he could be tied, he slipped on one side and was seized by three bystanders who swore that he should not be whipped and led him away in spite of the constable and with no small difficulty myself recovered the prisoner out of their hands and had the judgement executed."

About the same date as the above incident took place, a man living in Harbour Main district was charged with "having feloniously, wilfully and with malice aforethought, struck and wounded a resident of that district upon the head and with his hand or hands twisted the neck-cloth of the deceased"; he was charged also that he did "feloniously, wilfully and of malice aforethought so wound, bruise and strangle the deceased that he instantly died." The prisoner pleaded "Not Guilty." The charge was given to the jury, the Bailiff, who attended to the jury, being sworn to keep them without meat, drink, candle or lodging or suffering any person to speak to them until they were agreed on their verdict. The jury then withdrew. The sentence of the court was as follows: "That the prisoner, to the gaol in St. John's aforesaid from whence he came, should be sent back and there remain until tomorrow, twelve o'clock at noon, at which time before the Court House he should be burnt in the right hand with a hot iron, marked with the letter R, forfeit his goods and chattels, paying the charges of the court, etc., and be set at liberty."

In the district of Placentia and St. Mary's, a number of men were charged with having broken open the door of a resident and in a brutal manner having beaten two persons who were in the house at the time. They were sentenced to receive thirty-nine lashes each on the bare back and to find security for their keeping the peace for the future. A woman having been in their company was ordered to find security for her keeping the peace, and if at any time she was found guilty of such offenses, the justices of the peace ordered her to be whipped and sent out of the harbour."

Over thirty years ago, Judge Pinsent compiled some law reports of the happenings of those old days, a few of which I find of much interest. An individual who stole wood from his neighbour, it having been proved against him, was ordered to receive twelve lashes on the bare back at the customary place of punishment. Some persons who had entered the home of a man and his wife at Burin and beaten them were found guilty and ordered "that they should receive thirty-nine lashes each on the 20th day of March at the usual place of correction and be afterwards returned to jail. On the 21st of March to be brought again to the place of correction and receive 39 lashes in addition." A deserter from his master at Ferryland, and found thieving in Hr. Grace, was sentenced to receive forty lashes in two instalments and to be drawn through the harbour by a horse and then confined to jail until he could be sent back to his master at Ferryland. Judge Pinsent says, "The cat o' nine tails seems to have been admirably adopted to the case of a man who upon his wife's complaint was convicted of endeavouring to suffocate and otherwise ill-treating his children and of threatening his wife with a hatchet." This inhuman wretch received thirty-nine lashes on the bare back with imprisonment until he could find security for his good behaviour. In Bonavista, so the Judge says, "I observe a case in which a man, for supplying a person with liquor through a cell window, is committed to the stocks and another, prior to the ministration of the 'cats,' is to parade the settlement with a label on his back. A man who was accused and convicted of having stolen a quantity of rum was ordered to be led to the gallows with a halter round his neck and from thence to the whipping-place, there to be stripped and receive on his bare back thirty-nine lashes." A person having been proven guilty of stealing cabbage was ordered to pay the value to the owner and to walk round the town guarded by constables with cabbages tied round his neck.

When the faction fights[38] used to take place in St. John's, some lively times ensued. On one occasion (this was when Mr. Colclough[39] was Chief Justice), a number of men were arrested for having taken part in a faction fight and were fined and put in prison. The Judge, speaking about the fight, says of one of the prisoners, "I have ordered those who were only convicted of being in the crowd to be confined for one week each and to find ample security to keep the peace for three years, and one handsome and as fine a young man as I ever saw, who was convicted in two riots, to be publicly whipped tomorrow morning from Sawyer's Corner to the Court House for the first and confined for six months for the last offence, part of which I shall pardon as the support of his aged mother and sisters depends on his exertions."

In the early part of the last century, a person who held up another on the streets of St. John's and robbed him was sentenced to be hanged. The sentence was commuted to penal servitude. He was banished to New South Wales. A person who entered the home of another at Petty Harbour and stole one cloth jacket, one pair of cloth breeches and several other things was sentenced as follows: "The culprit was returned to the jail from whence he came; there he had to remain a few hours, and then he was taken to the public whipping post, where he received thirty-nine lashes on the bare back, and after paying the court fees he was set at liberty." Another individual who had stolen goods to the value of four pounds was transported and was warned that if he should return to Newfoundland he would be put to death. In 1809, a man sentenced to death for murder was ordered that before he should be executed he should be drawn on a sledge from the jail up King's Road to the Barrens, where he was hanged near the King's woodshed.

Lieut. Lawry was murdered in St. John's in 1750. He was lieutenant on HMS *Boston*. He was attacked while going to the homes of some men who had been impressed for the Navy; the men were rescued and the lieutenant was killed. His murderers were found and sentenced to be hanged. The hanging took place on the Barrens near the garrison. A diary kept at the time by an officer of the *Boston* says, in relation to the culprits, "There is a circumstance or two attending the execution of the two men I wish to mention, and that is relative to the dress of the hangman and the dress of the malefactors. An executioner is so detested in this country that were he known, he would entail disgrace on his posterity. The person who filled this office to the murderers of Mr. Lawry did his business in disguise. He wore a wig made of black sheep's wool, which covered his head and shoulders. He had a mask on and was covered with a large long cloak. The two culprits walked from the jail to the fatal spot. Each wore on his head a kind of bonnet or turban made of fine white linen, which contained three or four yards at least. The hangman, malefactors and priest walked in a group and were surrounded by military, who formed a very strong guard."

About 70 years ago, the late Hon. John Kent,[40] one-time Premier of Newfoundland, stated in the House of Assembly that the Rev. Denis Mackin, Parish Priest of Brigus, had written a most feeling letter as regards how justice was administered. It read as follows: "You would do a very agreeable and certainly a most laudable act by calling for the return of Luke Prendergast at our sessions here last October for stealing one turnip from Joshua Green, Esq., value sworn at one penny sterling, for which the poor child, only eight years old, had to undergo an imprisonment of three days in Harbour Grace jail. The circumstances of the case, as I am aware, are as follows: the child Prendergast, in company with a few more little creatures, went in from Cupids to collect a few brambles for firing, and he, in an innocent freak, ventured into the field of Joshua Green and took a turnip, which produced this severe dispensation of justice. I had almost forgotten to say that there is no fence to the field, and the owner had to employ a man to watch it day and night to prevent the trespassing of cattle and other animals. Nearly the whole day was spent in getting through this great trial, and it ended in ordering off, on charge of the constable, the poor child, who had to be put on horseback. The expense of hiring the horse and that of the constable must, of course, come out of the funds of the Colony."

The late Hon. Patrick Morris,[41] who with Dr. Carson[42] was the first to begin the struggle for a local government for Newfoundland, says as regards another miscarriage of justice, "A poor man in Bonavista had been charged with stealing cabbages from the garden of a stipendiary magistrate who immediately summoned him before himself and sentenced him to three months imprisonment in Trinity gaol. At the expiration of his confinement, the poor man was proceeding home when he lost his way and remained out for 3 or 4 days. The consequence was that he lost both his arms and legs, and he now remains a miserable object with his family. This was a most lamentable case, and the magistrate acted in profound ignorance of his duty." We ought to be thankful that in this country today we live in unity with our fellow-men and that the barbarous system of punishment which had marred the old days has passed away forever.

8

A Geology of St. John's

John Baird, **"Short Account of the Rocks in the Neighbourhood of St. John's, Newfoundland"**
Memoirs of the Wernerian Natural History Society
4 (1822): 151-56

In approaching the fishing grounds on the coast of America, the soundings were from sixty to thirty fathoms, over the great Bank of Newfoundland, generally about thirty-five. The lead [sounding] brought up a fine sand and frequently small pieces of rough flint, together with particles of a green smooth mineral in the form of coarse green sand. It is certainly a singular fact that so large a portion of shallow water should exist so far out to sea, the sea deepening so rapidly beyond the Bank. Is it not probable that a large tract of dry land had formerly existed where the bank is now found? The rocks which formed this land may have been composed of very soft materials, and the occurrence of flint and green sand over the Bank seems to indicate that the greater part of the original rocks had been of the Chalk and Green Sand Formations. A country composed of these rocks, which are of the latest formation, must have been very low, and in consequence much exposed to the action of the sea. By degrees the whole may have been inundated and entirely swept away, leaving the harder debris, the flint and green sand, to form the gravel at the bottom.

The coast round St. John's is bleak, bare and rocky, and almost everywhere precipitous. On both sides of St. John's harbour, perpendicular cliffs of trap-tuff rise to the height of three or four hundred feet. The interior of the country is hilly but does not rise to a great elevation, few of the hills being more than five or six hundred feet above the level of the sea. They are generally round-backed and frequently wooded to the top. The whole uninhabited part of the country is one immense forest, consisting chiefly of fir and birch. No extensive valleys or plains occur, but hill succeeds hill in almost unvarying succession. The physiognomy of the country is an elegant outline of hill and dale: the scenery, however, wants variety. Lakes are numerous over the whole island, as far as it is known, and many of them, near the coast, are large and beautiful. They occur even on the tops of the hills and are said to be often of great depth. The soil is in general light. Oats and barley thrive; and potatoes, turnips and other kitchen vegetables grow fully as well as in England. Summer weather in Newfoundland is short but warm and very favourable to vegetation. The winter is uncommonly severe, the spring and autumn very changeable. There is good pasture for cattle in ground that is cleared.

The passage into St. John's harbour, which in shape very much resembles a man's foot, is by a narrow entrance called The Narrows, which extends nearly east and west about half a mile. Both sides of this entrance are high, abrupt and rocky. The rocks are the same on each side, being continued across from the one to the other. I think there is little doubt that the opposite sides of the Narrows had once been joined. A rapid river runs into the harbour. The harbour itself, previous to the formation of the Narrows, may have been a lake. The river appears to have been once much larger. By the action of the sea without and of the river and lake within, the rent or chasm by which the river formerly emptied itself into the sea may have been gradually enlarged till it has attained its present size. The average width may be two or three hundred yards. Quidi Vidi (pronounced Kitty-Vitty) River and Lake may one day present an entrance and harbour similar to those of St. John's.

The mineralogy of the country round St. John's is very simple. The first rock, on entering the Narrows, is trap-tuff. This rock is distinctly stratified, each stratum generally measuring two or three feet in thickness. The strata lie N.E. and S.W., or rather N.E. by N. and S.W. by S. The dip is to the N.W. at an angle of from 70° to 80°. The basis of this rock consists chiefly of distinct grains or quartz, felspar and red claystone. The imbedded minerals or pebbles are, for the most part, of the same substances: felspar, common and compact, the latter with small imbedded grains of quartz; quartz, often of a slaty or fibrous structure; jasper, red claystone, bloodstone, hornstone &c. These imbedded minerals, at the foot of the hill or cliff (particularly the quartz and felspar), are generally from an inch to three inches in diameter and gradually decrease as we ascend; at the top of the hill, they rarely exceed the fourth part of an inch in diameter. Does not this fact countenance the mechanical disposition of the trap-tuff? This rock appears much harder than the common varieties of the trap-tuff which I have seen.

It is this rock which forms those precipitous cliffs on either side of the mouth of the Narrows. The opposite sides of the Narrows rise very rapidly from the sea to a considerable height. The highest part of the trap-tuff formation is about 300 feet above the sea, its thickness about 500 yards. The trap-tuff passes very gradually and most beautifully into the next rock, which is amygdaloid. In this passage of the one rock into the other, the stratified structure is still retained, one stripe or narrow stratum being distinctly marked trap-tuff, the next amygdaloid, the stripes of the former being broadest at first, gradually becoming narrower and less defined till the amygdaloidal rock entirely prevails.

The strata of the amygdaloid also run in the direction of N.E. by N. and S.W. by S. and dip likewise to the N.W. at an angle of about 65°. The basis of this rock, like that of the trap-tuff, consists of minute grains of quartz, felspar and claystone. The imbedded portions are invariably of a red, smooth, hard claystone: they seldom have the amygdaloidal form but are square or rhomboidal or in longish slates. The greater part of the amygdaloidal rock is entirely destitute of these portions, while, on the other hand, more than one half of some of the strata is composed of them. The amygdaloid is frequently distinctly stratified, each stratum being a few feet thick.

The trap-tuff and amygdaloid are both of a reddish colour; the latter, however, sometimes occurs of a grey colour. The greatest height of the amygdaloid formation is 500 feet; its thickness is about three or four hundred yards, extending from the top of Signal Hill to the foot of the Crow's Nest.

Resting upon the amygdaloid is found the greenstone, lower in height than the amygdaloid but higher than the trap-tuff. This rock extends from the foot of the Crow's Nest (it being of greenstone) to the foot of Signal Hill, or to the town of St. John's a thickness of six or seven hundred yards. The Crow's Nest, on which is built a small fort, is four hundred feet above the level of the sea. The principal constituent part of this rock is apparently felspar. Its most common colour is green, though sometimes grey and red; it is stratified and sometimes possesses a beautiful slaty structure. The strata of the greenstone also run N.E. and S.W.; their dip is to the N.W., at a much smaller angle than the preceding rock, the inclination not exceeding 50°.

Resting upon the greenstone we find the next rock claystone, the strata of which have the same direction and dip as the others, the angle of inclination, however, not being above 35° or 40°. The claystone formation extends two miles in thickness beyond the greenstone, occasionally alternating with strata of compact felspar, each stratum measuring from half a foot to a foot in thickness. The claystone being much softer than the rocks before described, the country where it prevails is also much lower. The town of St. John's is built upon the claystone. In colour, it is most frequently grey, often also brown, dark-brown, red, whitish and of other colours. It is often beautifully striped. It is fine-grained, smooth and often conchoidal in the fracture. The strata of this rock are occasionally columnar, which is also sometimes the case with the greenstone; and the columns are composed of round concentric balls.

The next rock, whose direction, dip and inclination are the same as those of the claystone, is compact felspar. This rock first alternates with the claystone and then prevails alone for above a mile. Being harder than the claystone, the country composed of it is higher. Its colour is also various, light and dark grey, greenish-grey, green, blue &c. It is translucent, or slightly translucent, on the edges, while the claystone is perfectly opaque. The compact felspar has a splintery conchoidal fracture; the fracture of the claystone, on the other hand, is even and always smooth. The compact felspar is more or less fine in the grain and the splinters more or less large. The strata of the compact felspar, like those of the greenstone and claystone, are also at times columnar, the columns being composed of small, round concentric balls, and very brittle. These balls are at times partially composed of hornstone. This mineral occurs also in the compact felspar in thin beds, in veins and in masses: its colour is green, its fracture smooth, conchoidal, it is slightly translucent on the edges and is as hard as quartz.

Claystone again succeeds the compact felspar, and the latter is again succeeded by the former, thus alternating for about eight or ten miles across the peninsula. The claystone always possesses a slaty structure and soon decays. The soil over the greenstone and amygdaloid is rich and good, while over the claytone and compact felspar it is light and poor.

9

A Captured Beothuk Female

"Curious Account of a Female Red Indian"
La Belle Assemblée; Or, Bell's Court and Fashionable Magazine,
128, 1 October 1819

Many attempts have been made to open up a friendly intercourse with the irascible Red Indians of Newfoundland, and the government lately offered a reward of fifty pounds to any person who should bring one of them alive to St. John's. At length a fisherman contrived to seize a young female who was paddling in her canoe to procure birds' eggs from an islet at a short distance from the mainland. This woman was immediately conveyed to the capital, the fisherman received his reward and the captive was treated with great humanity, kindness and attention.

The principal merchants and ladies of St. John's vied with each other in cultivating her good graces, and presents poured in upon her from all quarters. She seemed tolerably contented with her situation when surrounded by a company of female visitors but became outrageous if any man appeared, excepting the person who deprived her of her liberty, to him she was ever gentle and affectionate. Her body and hair were stained of a red colour, as it is supposed by juice extracted from the alder tree; and from their custom of dying the skin and hair the nation has acquired the appellation of Red Indians.

When this female had remained long enough at St. John's to be made perfectly sensible of the kindness and good intentions of the Europeans, the fisherman who brought her thither was desired to reconduct her to the spot where he had formerly dragged her away. The sequel of the story is so horrid that it would scarcely have been credited, had not the author of this account received it upon the testimony of many respectable persons in different parts of Newfoundland. The villain who had deprived this poor savage of her relations, her friends and her liberty conceived and actually carried into execution the diabolical scheme of murdering her on her voyage back in order to possess himself of those baubles which had been presented to her by the inhabitants of St. John's. By this barbarous act the monster obtained articles to the value of nearly a hundred pounds; and it is said that he has since retired to England to enjoy the plunder of his unfortunate victim![43]

10

Bishop Fleming's Account of the Status Quo in 1836

Michael Anthony Fleming (1792-1850) was the Roman Catholic bishop of St. John's principally responsible for changing a small mission into four parishes and a large diocese of over 40,000 congregants.

Michael Anthony Fleming,
"Catholic Mission of Newfoundland"
Weekly Orthodox Journal, 1836, 201-5

To the Very Rev. Dr. Spratt
Carmelite Convent, Dublin
Very Rev. and Very Dear Sir,

Having at length closed the narrative of my visitation of the south-western portion of Newfoundland, it is my intention now to conclude these letters with a brief detail of the painful circumstances connected with the mission which occurred since my return to St. John's in order that from them such information may be gleaned as will give a correct estimate of the state of the wants of our truly interesting congregation and may even suggest an idea of the best mode of supplying them.

Your valuable present of books, together with those you have been so kind as to send with them, amounting to about four hundred volumes, including prayer books, catechisms &c. which we owe to the benevolence of other charitable individuals in Dublin, reached me only a few days before I sailed. In this extensive collection I found a parcel having the name of that zealous, talented and most useful labourer in the vineyard, the Rev. Wm. Walsh, another of that indefatigable patriot of civil and religious liberty, Mr. Battersby, many with the name of Mr. Davis and several dozens bearing the name of James Lynham – perhaps the same gentleman from whom I have had the pleasure of receiving a letter a few days ago evincing a zeal on behalf of the object of my mission to this country that entitles him to the ardent prayers of my poor people and to my grateful acknowledgements.

Although these books were intended by the pious benefactors for the use of the convent school, as I had been myself supplying that establishment, I thought I should not be departing far from the gratification of their or your wishes if I distributed them amongst a people who reside far from St. John's and who have neither means nor opportunity to procure these devotional aids.

I took these, therefore, with me on my visitation; and when added to those which I myself had purchased expressly for the purpose, the entire number of books with which I was provided exceeded six thousand, all of which I distributed on my way wherever I thought them most needed, and wherever they reached they were received with the deepest gratitude and with heartfelt blessings and prayers for the benevolent individuals who, though at two thousand miles distance, sympathize in their wants, and with people so gratefully disposed they cannot fail to effect great good. Books are, in this country, of inestimable value. Even in comparatively contracted districts the communication between the several harbours is often so uncertain that the poor people are compelled to be many weeks together without seeing their priests, and many harbours, as I have observed in my former letters, are left for years without once seeing a clergyman.

The clergyman in Tilting Harbour, for instance, is confined to that spot during the entire winter and cannot relieve, either by instruction or the sacraments, any of the inhabitants of the harbours adjacent: while his parish clergyman resident in King's Cove is, during the same lapse of time, confined to that neighbourhood; and between the residences of the parish priest and the curate, a space of perhaps two or three hundred miles as you wind along the shore from harbour to harbour, is, from the close of September or the middle of October till about the tenth of the following June, utterly neglected, and the entire of Green Bay to the northward and Trinity Bay to the southward in the same district similarly circumstanced.

In many of the harbours in these places, they have little chapels in which the inhabitants assemble every Sunday and offer up such prayers as to them seem suitable, or as they are instructed by the clergyman to use upon such occasions; and where there are no chapels they assemble in a private house. Only imagine, then, the great value, to poor people so situated, of books conveying practical instructions in religion and morality; and yet do we find it utterly impossible to meet their great want, although, through your benevolent assistance, I have been enabled to effect much good in that way upon this late occasion.

As I remarked in the close of my last letter, I found my poor people, upon my landing in St. John's, sunk in the greatest misery, owing to the ravages making among them by the smallpox; and as upon the breaking out of every epidemic, it is the humbler classes whose poverty invited disease – the poor of St. John's were sufferers indeed.

At this time, too, the utmost anxiety pervaded the public mind because now approached the period at which the labours of the fishery came to a close and when those who had toiled through a long summer naturally expected to meet a recompense in the same manner as they had been accustomed at all times before: that is, from the merchant for whose advantage they had been toiling. And here observe that the fishing servants form the most numerous class of the population in St. John's, numbering over four thousand.

The person who hires the fishing servants is called a planter, and although not really the steward of the merchant yet has always been regarded as acting in that capacity, and therefore the fish and oil procured during the season through the labour of the servant has ever been made liable in the merchant's hands for the servants' wages; or where the amount of fish &c. taken was insufficient, then for a rateable proportion of the proceeds, because the planter is most commonly a man destitute of means to defray the expense, as the steward of a nobleman could not be imagined to be a sufficient security for the wages of the servants he engaged. This has been always the mercantile usage on the subject of servants' wages, and it has been strengthened by repeated acts of parliament and confirmed by numberless decisions of the courts of sessions and of the supreme court under the administration of Chief Justice Reeves, Forbes and Tucker; but on the coming in of Judge Boulton[44] he reversed the principle and exonerated the merchant from a claim, which relieved several of them of many hundred pound wages and involved the wretched people in a proportionate degree of misery and destitution.

At the time to which I allude, the Hon. Chief Justice was in London, and the utmost anxiety pervaded the poor people to ascertain whether the next circuit court would relieve them; but, upon the court opening, it began to be rumoured that the chief judge was returning, and therefore Judge Brenton actually refused to entertain a single civil case lest this question should be called up, for he had often and often decided it the other way before Judge Boulton's time; therefore it lay over till Judge Boulton landed, and in a few days a final decision dashed the cup of hope from the lips of many thousands who, with their families, were looking to his fiat for means of support while they saw their little ones dying around them of a loathsome disease.

Here was a trying occasion for the clergyman who possessed humanity to calm the feelings of a father who saw his offspring perishing with want after passing the summer in toil and hardship many hundred miles from home to enrich an individual who now took an advantage of his situation. In justice, however, to the commercial body in St. John's, I ought to mention that the greater proportion of them scorned to take advantage of that adjudication and have paid with cheerfulness their servants' full demand, an act of benevolence which will be long and gratefully remembered by the poor people.

But to make such an individual as the one above described respect the laws of his country, to convince him that he ought to respect the constituted authorities under whom he had suffered such wrong, could only be effected by mitigating the affliction and soothing the wounded spirit of the individual; and the priest succeeded in restraining them from the commission of acts of violence or outrage so far, that never in the history of Newfoundland has there been known less crime to have been committed in St. John's than during the past winter.

To add to the difficulties of this period, so very many persons who had previously been vaccinated, and some more than once, had fallen victims upon this occasion to smallpox that all confidence in the efficacy of the vaccine matter, as a preventive, was destroyed, and at all sides they began to inoculate with the natural virus. The number of cases, as stated upon the evidence of the practising medical men before the grand jury, amounted to upwards of 6,000 in St. John's.

About the first week of November, the disease broke out in Petty Harbour, one of the villages of the district of St. John's, which place I mentioned before as having been the first port I put into on setting out for the southward; and as this place is entirely occupied by people engaged in the fishery, and probably ninety-nine hundreds of them fishing servants, I at once saw that their extreme poverty would preclude the possibility of procuring medical assistance and that, for the same reason, I knew they could not provide either the necessary medicines or needful nutriment.

In such an emergency, what was to be done? The executive had attempted nothing to check the disease or to soften the visitation upon the poor. There were 6,000 or 7,000l. in colonial coffers excess over the year's expenditure and debt, and yet not one single farthing was given to relieve the sufferings of the afflicted. There was no hospital opened, no dispensary instituted or recommended, no soup house founded, not a subscription opened even though some five or six and twenty thousand pounds sterling of salaries are paid annually out of the public taxes to persons resident principally at St. John's; but the work of death was progressing, and the terrors of pestilence blanched every cheek.

Nay, there seemed to be arts used, I will not say to spread the contagion but to add to the apprehensions of the public and to increase their fears. The chief judge on the bench declared it the duty of the grand jury to indict anyone who came out of a house where persons lay ill of smallpox and actually in open court reproved Mr. Harding, a respectable citizen living at the Beach, whose amiable and highly accomplished daughter was lying ill of the disease, for having come out of his house, even though he had done so in obedience to a summons of the court to attend upon the jury; and such a doctrine, at a moment when hundreds were going from door to door begging old linen for their children, their parents, their wives or their husbands – or food or clothing or other comforts necessary to the sick or the convalescent – was calculated to produce much discontent. In a few weeks, however, the disease visited the hon. judge's family, and he appeared abroad, breaking through the rules he himself had made.

But I have said that nothing was done to check the disease; I was wrong in saying so, for as soon as ever it began to attack the families of the respectable inhabitants, the physicians were invited to attend gratuitously at a house formerly occupied by the St. John's charity school, and for which no rent is payable, for the purpose of vaccinating the poor. At this time there were upwards of 2,000 or 3,000 persons, after having undergone inoculation with the natural matter, and when the disease exhibited itself as on the decline. However, on the opening of the House of Assembly, the Governor, in his speech, asked for a grant of money to stem the progress of smallpox, and a sum of 500l. was granted sometime in March or April, when not one case existed in St. John's.

Upon its breaking out in Petty Harbour, I went to that little place, and as I was unwilling to subject the excellent family of Mr. Reily, where I usually lodged (and where for the last forty years bishops and priests have always received a warm, welcome, comfortable and hospitable home), to the danger of infection through me, I resisted their kind entreaties to reside with them and begged the use of a waste house near our church: here I planted my medicine chest and set it up as the village dispensary, and here I staid for the remainder of the winter.

I now applied myself sedulously to the improvement of this interesting little harbour. I was engaged, as I remarked before, in erecting a beautiful little church, for here is a congregation of about 700 persons; and as the cemetery was in the very centre of the little town, I was solicitous to remove it to some place where sufficient soil to cover the bodies may be had – for as three persons who died of that dreadful disease had been interred before I came, I was apprehensive that danger might arise from leaving them there and allowing others to be buried in some instances within three or four yards of the doors of the houses.

The vicinity having been explored, a place perfectly suitable, and at about half a mile distance, was discovered, and to it I had all the bodies forthwith removed.

At my own expense I purchased a piece of ground adjoining the old cemetery in order to make it a useful square for the public around our church, and at great expense, by blasting the rocks, reduced it to a level so that it forms quite an embellishment in a little place where there is not a single level spot of six yards square in any other part of the harbour.

In fact, what with the building of the church, the purchasing ground and the clearing and levelling, &c. &c., I had expended upon that small town upwards of 800l, yet did it tend to bring great annoyance upon me. What was my surprise to learn one day from the Governor, upon the occasion of my waiting on him, that some of the Protestants of Petty Harbour had just petitioned against me! I then found that they had been worked upon – for they and I had always been on terms of friendship, nor did I make any difference between Protestant and Catholic in my attentions to the sick or in the gratuitous diffusion of medicine and nourishing food.

The Protestants, then, I had just found, had been worked upon to get this petition up to prevent my finishing the churchyard or square, for its professed object was to forbid my removing or interrupting the repose of the mortal remains of some of their deceased friends. Even Governor Prescott[45] himself must have seen through this and considered it got up from party motives, for in his reply to my official explanation of the subject, he recommended my waiting until those prejudices should be removed by remonstrances; and I am sure it is to his Excellency

I owe it, almost immediately were they removed, and one of their clergymen, I understand, was pleased to applaud my motives and admit that what I had done was for the improvement of the condition of the people.

I now withdrew from Petty Harbour and began to make arrangements for administering confirmation in my own district, preparatory to my departure from Newfoundland to solicit at Downing Street a grant of ground for the erection of a church and public school in St. John's &c. – not a single favour of the kind, not a grant of ground for any public purpose having ever been given by the government to the Catholics of Newfoundland – and on Monday the 25th of April, I had the satisfaction of administering the sacrament of Confirmation to 1,390 persons, principally children, in the church of St. John's.

And here allow me to say a word before I close upon our invaluable sisters of the Presentation Convent. Upon them devolved the onerous task of instructing upwards of 800 females of every age and preparing them for that holy sacrament, a task which, added to their usual avocations and occupying every instant of their time from morning until night, had not failed to make inroads upon tender constitutions already much injured by the incessant labour attendant upon their school, where so great a number of children were attended by so few nuns, as that all must be constantly employed. Never were individuals admitted to a sacrament better instructed, and never was the demeanour of such a multitude so truly edifying as on the morning of Confirmation.

On the following Sunday, 1st May, I confirmed 602 in Torbay; on the Sunday following, May 8th, 449 were confirmed in Portugal Cove, and on Sunday the 15th, 413 were admitted to the same sacrament in Petty Harbour – thus making a total in this district of 2,854, amongst whom were 304 converts to the faith, including the children of those converts.

On Friday, May 27th (this was Ember Week), I set out from St. John's at seven o'clock a.m. for Portugal Cove in order to consecrate the church of St. Patrick at Brigus, at the other side of Conception Bay; as it was so early, the Rev. Edward Troy and I, with two or three lay gentlemen who accompanied us, forbore to take our collation [light meal] before we left town, and when we arrived at the Cove the wind was so inviting that, promising as it did a passage of only two or three hours, we preferred starting immediately and stepped on board, having just barely broken our fast.

This may give you some idea of the uncertainty of the communication in this country. There was not on board the packet either meat or drink, for what need of either where you could see the landing place before you; but having been becalmed and headed by the wind afterwards, we were tossed about the bay that entire day, the entire of the night following, nor did we arrive at our destination till 11 o'clock a.m. next day, when we landed in a complete state of exhaustion from want of food.

I shall not tarry to describe the true Irish welcome we met from the people of Brigus or their truly good pastor the Rev. Denis Mackin; suffice it that we continued wind-bound here for several days after the consecration and that on the occasion of that ceremony there assembled people of all creeds from the most distant parts of the bay, so that so great a multitude of people had never before assembled in that part of the country.

I had arranged to consecrate, on the following Sunday, June the 5th, the beautiful church of Corpus Christi at Torbay, erected almost solely at the expense of the Rev. Edward Troy, a missionary than whom this country has never seen one more zealous or more ardently devoted to the duties of his sacred calling. We therefore sailed the first favourable moment and on that day consecrated this church for a truly good congregation.

And now one more duty remained to be fulfilled before my departure, for I had long promised the people of Harbour Grace to take the earliest opportunity of administering confirmation to them. In order to comply, I sailed on Tuesday the 7th, again accompanied by the Rev. Edward Troy, for Carbonear; and here I arrived in a few hours and on Wednesday confirmed upwards of 600 persons in Harbour Grace, amongst whom were many converts; but as the next day was wet, I thought that children could not well be brought on that morning from a distance. I therefore put off the confirmation at Carbonear till Friday, when 700 persons were admitted to participate in that sacrament, immediately after which we set sail for the Cove and arrived in St. John's on the same evening. As upon my arrival I found that several persons who had been disappointed on the former occasion were now well prepared here, on Whit-Sunday I confirmed 400 individuals, making the total in the district of St. John's 3,254.

I have thus brought this narrative down to the period of my departure; and I pray ardently and earnestly before my God that these details may tend to induce attention to the spiritual wants of an interesting but long neglected people and awaken the good and the wealthy to the spiritual distress of thousands of souls who are wandering without a shepherd around the snows of Labrador and on the bleak coasts of Newfoundland.

Believe me, with sentiments of esteem, your devoted and humble servant in Christ,

† Michael Anthony Fleming

11

The Aftermath of the Fire of 1846

"Return of Prosperity After a General Fast
[extract of a letter from the Rev. John Brewster]"
Wesleyan Missionary Notices
New Series 5, No. 105, September 1847

I love to be the bearer of good tidings. I am the happiest when, with David, I can say, "My heart is inditing a good matter."[46] After twelve months' suffering from fire, tempest and famine, we who can discern "the signs of the times" mark the footsteps of Jehovah in the deep waters and sing,

> Whatever ills the world befall,
> A pledge of endless good we call,
> A sign of Jesus near.[47]

We are anxiously waiting for the sanctification of our national calamities and for the outpouring of the Holy Spirit. We see the signs of good in St. John's. Our people are truly humbled. Our congregations are large and attentive. The prayer meetings, the week-night preaching, but particularly the class meetings are well attended. A few backsliders have been restored to God. Our financial affairs are unusually good: while all has been tempestuous and adverse without, peace and prosperity have been within our palaces. Join with us in offerings of praise unto God!

When his Excellency Sir J. Gaspard Le Marchant,[49] our Governor, landed in St. John's last April, he was struck with astonishment at the wretched appearance of the town. The work of destruction by the late fire was everywhere visible. Besides this, the storm of the 19th of September last strewed the coasts with the wrecks of many a hardy fisherman's property. Their winter's provisions were lost. The potatoes had failed; what few were saved were destroyed by the frost, which set in much earlier and keener. The starving population were driven from our out-harbours by famine. Loud cries of distress assailed our ears from every part. The Government-house was daily thronged by petitioners for relief. His Excellency proposed a public fast; and Wednesday, June 9th, the anniversary of the great fire, was fixed upon. I need not say how willingly we, as Wesleyan Ministers, united to make prayer unto God, deprecating his wrath and supplicating his mercy. The fast-day was devoutly and universally observed by the Protestants. The shops and merchants' stores were closed, the Protestant places of worship were opened early in the morning and filled with truly devout and weeping worshippers. It was a day of deep humiliation before God. The services of the sanctuary were of the most solemn and affecting character. Popery, of course, refused to join us, alleging its reason, "No faith in worship with heretics." But all who believe in and worship God as he is revealed in the Holy Scriptures will remember the fast-day of the 9th of June, 1847, with feelings of holy grief and joy.

Let the infidel world ridicule that great duty of Christianity as it pleases: we know who has said, "Seest thou how Ahab humbleth himself before me?"[50] and I am happy in recording that to which I was an eye and ear witness. After preaching in St. John's in the morning, I went to preach at Portugal Cove in the evening. I saw an unusual expression of pleasure on the countenances of our people and asked if they had felt it well with their souls that day. They answered, "It is well for the body as for the soul; for never, in our memory, have we seen such shoals of fish come up from the sea as we have seen today." Being rather doubtful, I determined to inquire of others. Accordingly, on the Saturday following, I rode off to another fishing settlement, Pouch Cove; and here I found them all in excellent spirits. "We never saw the like," said they. I stayed all night and proceeded by water to preach at Cape St. Francis, where we have a number of people engaged in the fishery. It seemed as if the sea were alive with the vast shoals of fish. I found our people at the Cape expressing their gratitude to God for such an abundant supply of the necessaries of life.

12

Agriculture in 1848

Hugh Alexander Emerson (d.1860) was called to the Newfoundland bar in 1829. He was first elected to the House of Assembly in 1837 and from 1837 to 1854 was Solicitor General.

Hon. H.A. Emerson,
"Agricultural Improvement in Newfoundland"
Simmonds's Magazine, 15 (1848): 393-94

St. John's,
28th October
My Dear Sir:

I promised you, in my last letter, that I would furnish you with some details respecting this depository of fish and fog, but, the Government not yet having received the returns from the various outports, I am not in a position, at the present time, to enter upon the subject as I could wish; however, I shall be glad, and perhaps it may hereafter conduce to your interests, that you let something like the following extract appear in your next magazine.

An uninterrupted residence of nearly seventeen years in the island enables me to say, without fear of contradiction, that Sir

Gaspard Le Marchant has effected more real, substantial and practical good in the course of eighteen months than any governor who ever administered the affairs of Newfoundland; but more particularly do I allude to his three immediate predecessors [Sir Thomas Cochrane, Capt. Henry Prescott and Major General Sir John Harvey]. His Excellency early saw our true condition. With a large and rapidly increasing population – with a declining revenue and no domestic resources, an increased taxation must be the inevitable result of our slumbering and apathetic industry. He therefore roused the attention of the inhabitants to the imperative necessity of a practical experiment in the growing of wheat, and I am most happy to say that his efforts have proved eminently successful.

He has dispelled the error under which the inhabitants of this fine colony have so long laboured – namely, that our climate was uncongenial to the growth and ripening of wheat grain – and has abundantly proven that we may as successfully cultivate that crop as any of our western neighbours. His Excellency set the example of this triumphant effort by turning the untilled Government grounds into wheat fields, and, carrying with him the energies of a willing and industrious people, he has broken down the fence of ignorance, boldly entered the course and shown the rural population of Newfoundland that they, at least, may "seize the plough and greatly independent live."[51] I may safely say, we have now fairly tested the important question and that doubt no longer lingers on the brow of the husbandmen. Our temperature, too, during the past summer, was much in favour of the experiment, as it was, upon an average, four degrees lower than it had been for the last three years.

You may readily imagine my surprise, on returning to St. John's, to find the whole of its suburban parts one entire wheat field and that the potato and turnip crops, which had hitherto been our only production, had generally disappeared and their places supplied by the golden wheat sheaf. It was with no niggardly or sparing hand that our excellent Governor commenced this truly important experiment. To those who were in indigent circumstances and unable to purchase seed, it was given to them by the Government, and where there was any deficiency amongst those who were in a position to make the trial upon their own responsibility it was supplied, upon the payment of costs and charges in kind, at the conclusion of the season. The crops were generally got in from the middle of April to the middle of May and were as generally housed by the middle of September, well ripened, well filled and with an average return varying from 10 to 12, so that, with the average summer heat being against us, I may again say, we have fairly tested the important experiment and most satisfactorily succeeded.

There is one fact, and no unimportant one, I had almost forgotten to advert to, namely, that our wheat and barley crops have proved much safer than our oats, for whilst the first have ripened with vigour and health, the last have proved rather weakly and sickly during the last season, which shows a decided preference in the climate in favour of the wheat and barley. Our mills, too, must not be overlooked. We have now three in the neighbourhood of St. John's upon a most respectable scale, and as you may imagine, all in full operation; so that where, heretofore, indifference and apathy prevailed, a thriving competition and energy is rearing its head, and I have every reason to believe that, ere long, we shall be enabled to say to our neighbours we, too, have sown the seeds and are reaping the fruits of agricultural independence.

With success and promise before us, our untiring Governor has not overlooked our ultimate requirements; he has carefully and prudentially arranged for our further labour by ordering supplies of different seed wheat, the growth of Russia, Poland, Scotland, England and the Canadas, in order that when the proper time arrives, our infant strides in agriculture may not be defeated by the want of means to follow up our hitherto successful intentions.

Such, then, is our present condition under our able and indefatigable Governor; a powerful and successful impetus has been given to a branch of rural industry which will vitally affect the domestic comforts and the independence of a very large proportion of the inhabitants of Newfoundland who, before the arrival of His Excellency, were entangled in the web of dependence and poverty. Until the mists and misconceptions regarding the capabilities of the country were removed by his practical example, the husbandman of this fine colony toiled and laboured in gloomy despair and dissatisfaction; but he now joyfully hies him to the field "with the secret and cheering prospect of a farmer's independence."

13

Social Life in the 1840s and 1850s

H.F. Shortis, **"Random Jottings of By-gone Days"**
Papers of H.F. Shortis, Provincial Archives of Newfoundland and Labrador, vol. 2, 367

It is one of the privileges of mature life to look back on former days and contrast the manners and customs of those days with these of the present. As men grow old they become more or less reminiscent, and I propose to recall some of the manners and customs of St. John's in the late forties and middle fifties of the past century. My jottings will be erratic and discursive, as I have no data to guide me, and propose merely to record customs and events as they come up to me from retrospect.

It must be borne in mind that in the early fifties St. John's, although the commercial centre of activity in Newfoundland, was by no means the leader of fashion as understood today. In those days we had two distinct classes in St. John's, namely, the Fishermen and the "Quality" – the latter was the select and exclusive circle. In those days, St. John's was a military station, and, as a matter of course, the officers and their wives set the pace in society matters. Those who had access to this exclusive set were high government officials, members of the legal and medical profession, certain selected shopkeepers and civil servants whose salaries were not under £250 a year. In those days in St. John's, £250 (equalling our $1,000) was a fabulous sum for a man to be drawing regularly. Those, with their wives and families tacked on to the officers of Fort William and Fort Townshend, constituted the elite of all Newfoundland. One would think that, viewed from the standpoint of today, most people were well-to-do, were ambitious to get access to this exclusive circle. This is not the case. At any time there was another and altogether different aristocracy in St. John's – aristocracy of fishermen.

It must be remembered that at the time I write of, the fisheries were the all-prevailing and only industry in Newfoundland, and a well-to-do planter held a higher place in the popular esteem than even the Representative of Royalty itself. They were a noble and fearless race of men who gloried in their calling, whose life from the cradle to the grave was one continual battle with the elements, and it must be admitted that those were the Vikings who laid the foundation of our prosperity and to whom we owe all that we have and all that we shall have in the future. It is glorious for us Newfoundlanders to know that their descendants today are keeping up the best traditions of their sires on the Dreadnaughts[52] and battleships in the North Sea or on the broad Atlantic.

In the days I speak of, it was an impossibility to meet a fisherman, either young or old, on the streets of St. John's in the months of March, July or August. No young man especially would think of being seen at home during these months. Such an event would be looked upon as an everlasting disgrace. When a boy, I remember the following story going the rounds. A young fellow, fonder of a spree than work, having obtained his "crop" in the spring of the year, failed to turn up, and his master had to go on the voyage without him. He was subsequently rounded up and brought before the court. The judge, a stern old disciplinarian, in passing sentence upon him remarked that his term of imprisonment would expire at mid-summer and "then," he remarked, "what will you think of yourself on having to walk the streets of St. John's at that time of the year?" The judge made this appeal to his sentiments, thinking it would have more effect upon him than the fact of his imprisonment: so it would on the ordinary young man of the day, but this fellow was equal to the occasion, and he coolly remarked, "Well, Your Honour, I'll come in handy for going to funerals." The old judge was disgusted at his want of sentiment and self-respect, and he replied, "If people were called upon to attend your funeral, the community would not miss you much."

Leaving out the "Quality," there were three distinct classes in St. John's – the fishermen, the mechanics were tolerated and at social occasions fraternized with the fishermen, but the line was drawn at the "counter jumpers"; this was the title they gave the clerks in the various stores. The mechanics often availed themselves of the opportunity to go to the fishery in the summertime. This was especially so in the case of the coopers, who, for some unexplained reason, were prime favorites with the fishing population. In those days, there was not a "room" [fishing station] on the West Coast that could not boast of having two or three coopers on its staff. Trap fishing was unheard of at that time, but the cod seine was in the zenith of its glory. The duration of this fishery was from six to eight weeks; the work while it lasted was arduous and continuous but remunerative in the extreme, and as a result this branch of the industry absorbed all the spare coopers to be found in the city. This was lucky for the coopers, as during that season of the year there was practically no employment for coopers in St. John's.

In the case of the shipwrights, blacksmiths and sailmakers, matters were quite different, as during the summer months there was always employment for that class of men. The tailors, although a very necessary class of men, did not stand high in the popular favour. This may be accounted for by the fact that nearly all the clothing then in use was imported from “home,” meaning, of course, the British Isles. As a matter of plain fact, the tailor of that day stood only one degree higher in public esteem than the unfortunate “counter jumper.” I am inclined to think that the style of dress the tailors affected, being very near the approach of the “jumpers’” outfit, has much to do with their unpopularity in society.

Even in those far-off days, the cut of one’s coat had very much to do with his status in society. The “reefer” was the all-prevailing outer garment to adorn the manly person, and anyone deviating in the slightest degree from this style of coat was likely to find himself cast into outer darkness to foregather with the “jumper” and the tailor.

My object is to try and give the people of these days an outline of how their forebears went through life, under what conditions they worked, the remuneration they received, the condition of the city at the time, the contentment of its people and a general faithful portrayal of how the foundations of the present prosperity of our city were laid down.

As I stated at the commencement of these notes, I do not claim to set forth dates for the facts herein stated, nor will there be any effort made to state consecutively every event and incident related. Facts, circumstances and events will be related as they come up to memory, and in describing conditions, manners and customs, I shall be careful to avoid, endeavouring to prove why these existed. I should leave all these things to the political economist and speculation philosopher, whose province it is to enquire into these things, and show cause as to why they existed and point out remedies and thus prove how they could have been evident. My object is to point out facts, not to show what gave rise to them.

It is surprising, in looking back, to see what can be accomplished in one lifetime. I, in my day, have seen surgery in its infancy in Newfoundland; I have seen phlebotomy[53] practiced and have known the extraction of a tooth a matter of more serious importance than an operation for appendicitis at the present day. Later on, I shall have something to say on the subject of surgical operations in my day.

I have witnessed the evolution of dress in our maternal ancestors. I have seen the comfortable and serviceable paisley shawl tightly fitting about the throat and the "puke" bonnet made of warm and serviceable material give place to the modern flimsy and open-breasted dress and light-textured and fashionable hats, and incidentally have seen the phenomenal increase of consumption in every successive generation.

I have seen the schoolmistress in St. John's in the prime and zenith of her glory. I have sat at the feet of the old-time pedagogue and have suffered from the infliction of his ferrule. I have seen the sanitary conditions of St. John's such as would vie with a Chinese and Turkish slum. As a result, I well remember the days when we had those hardy annuals – typhus, typhoid and smallpox – visiting us every year with a regularity that was monotonous, and the advent of December brought those unwelcome visitors to the city with unfailing precision.

I have seen all those conditions pass away. The schoolmistress and antiquated pedagogue gave place to institutions of modern and refined education. Primitive and unwholesome sanitary conditions have been swept away before the march of scientific improvements. I am thankful to state epidemics of the nature referred to above are mercifully the exception and not the rule, as in the days of which I speak.

I fancy I hear some pessimistic youth exclaim that this must be a centenarian old fossil who is taking in this strain. Not at all! All those things and more have happened in my time, and I claim to be still on the bright and breezy side of seventy. Nevertheless, I am more than surprised, in looking back and viewing in retrospective moments, the wonderful improvements that have been wrought in this my native city since my boyhood days.[54]

I have seen St. John's a military station. I have seen the two forts occupied by troops. The first military contingent I remember was the Royal Newfoundland Company. Those were hardy and tried veterans. The time of many of them expired while in this colony, and few, if any of them, went back to the Old Country. They married and settled down here. Many of their descendants are at present in St. John's, but the greater part of them are to be found in the outports.

On the withdrawal of the Royal Newfoundland Co., their place was supplied by a contingent from the 62nd Infantry Regiment, a magnificent bond of men in the prime and vigor of manhood, most of whom were decorated with clasps and medals won at the Crimea.[55] The battalion was composed of English, Irish and Scotch, the latter predominant. The 62nd remained about four years and were then withdrawn to give place to a mixed contingent composed of the Royal Canadian Rifles and a company of Royal Artillery, the former being quartered at Fort William and the latter at Fort Townshend. After two years' service, the Artillery were withdrawn, but the Rifles remained until the military were finally withdrawn altogether from the Colony. Just at present, I am unable to recall the circumstances that led up to the recall of the forces from Newfoundland and leaving us without adequate protection. Many of the officers of both branches of the service intermarried into the first families of the city, and some of their descendants are serving with distinction in the present World War.

Responsible government is a product of my most youthful days. They were stormy and troublesome days for the aspiring politician. The men on the unpopular side ran serious risks, and during an election contest their personal safety was a matter of grave concern to them. St. John's and Harbour Main carried off the palm for stormy elections. Those were the days of the open vote, and every man knew how his neighbour voted. They were courageous and fearless men and knew how to stand by and back up their convictions. They feared no threat and were regardless of consequences when they went into the booth to record their votes.

Few people now living in St. John's remember the old-time "hustings," not the temporary structure of comparative recent date. I mean the old-time and substantial erections, one of which was, from the first dawn of political contests, erected on a prominent site on Queen Street and the other at the head of the King's Beach. These two sections became historic as the site of the "hustings" as the elections came around. During the excitement of the elections, feelings ran high and strong passions were aroused. Then, as now, appeals were made to the lowest passions of the human heart, often with the resultant aftermath of broken heads and tender bones: but with all, the redeeming quality remained; there was no animosity or ill-feeling retained. The hatchet of war was buried till the next election came round.

Those old-time candidates were fine fellows, full of moral and physical courage. They entered the contest to win, and no matter how the fortunes of the day went on, for or against them, they stood by their colors and invariably fought to the finish. The "hustings" were erected a fortnight before polling day and had to be substantially built, as many a rough encounter took place on its platform, and if it gave way the consequences would prove serious. Fully matured eggs were an important factor in the conduct of an election in those days and were used as a medium of interchange of courtesies between the opposing parties. I well remember, as a very small boy in McLea's election,[56] being standing on Queen Street, listening to the oratory of Talbot, Renouf and Casey when a prominent and influential merchant who happened to be blessed with a very voluminous beard opened his mouth to make a speech: the cavity was instantly filled by one of those highly flavored spheroids, and the contents therefrom streaming down his capacious whiskers made his presence a very ludicrous appearance. All this is changed today, and although the same amount – and more – of duplicity and deception is practiced, the rough and tumble element is almost entirely eliminated.

Few people in St. John's know what a "truckleymuck" is. This was a small, two-wheeled cart drawn by two or more dogs, used by the people of the nearby extern settlements to bring into town such merchandise as fresh herring, salmon, lobsters, etc., and in those days this was not the exceptional but principal mode of conveyance for such commodities as I have mentioned, and on Saturdays, which were then as now the principal market days, in certain sections of the city the sidewalks were often blocked with those small trucks and the dogs stretched under them enjoying a needed rest after their long and tiresome journey.

In the early and up to the middle of the fifties, a milk cart was a rare thing to be seen in the city. The farmers of the country settlements, those English, Irish and Scotch pioneers to whom we owe so much, would consider it an outrage to take away a home and man from their legitimate duties, namely, hauling wood for fuel, reclaiming the forest, collecting peat for fertilizing purposes, for the less remunerative purpose of supplying milk to the folks of the city. There was a special man kept on every farm for the purpose of bringing the milk into town. His duties, especially in wintertime, were far from being a sinecure. This class of man was looked upon as being a sort of institution in those days. In the different sections in which he served, he was known by his Christian name as Jimmy the milkman, Paddy the milkman, etc., etc.

Fewer still of your readers remember that style of conveyance known as the "panniers." The "panniers" were two square boxes, something shorter but very much deeper than the ordinary cracker boxes. These were strapped together by stout and broad bands of brin, of much the same material as the bags containing Hamburg bread, which was imported in such large quantities up to the seventies. The pony or horse was a *rara avis* in most of the outports in those days, but I have seen, in my youthful days, once or twice a week a horse from Portugal Cove or Torbay laden with "panniers," that is the two boxes I have mentioned, thrown over the horse's or pony's back and each box laden with salmon, cod, herring or lobsters.

It is a sad commentary on the present-day feverish desire to amass riches, and still more to call to mind with what content and satisfaction those simple fishers prepared to return to their homes, many of them well up in years, having travelled some seven, some nine miles, then cheerfully undertaking to go back over the same road, being enriched by their day's toil in the sum of three to four dollars. These are facts hard to understand, no doubt, in the light of present-day conditions.

14

A Trip from Canada

"Portia," "A Trip to Newfoundland"

The Week: A Journal for Men and Women, 29 July 1886, 563-65

The dense grey cloud which had been hanging over the ocean since early dawn and surrounding all objects in impenetrable gloom cleared up, as if by magic, the instant the steamer Norwegian passed between the two grim sentinel rocks that guard the entrance to St. John's harbour, and in a burst of sunlight the picturesque capital of Newfoundland was revealed to our view.

I had been up and on deck since five o'clock that morning, taking observations on the weather and harassing the sailors with questions displaying a lamentable ignorance of nautical affairs, also trying to discern through the mist some portion of the dimly defined coastline. The fog obliged us to keep well out to sea, but my investigations were rewarded now and then by glimpses of grim, rocky promontories, looming gigantically up in unexpected places. The impression I thus received of the country was not cheering. I stood beside my stepfather, near the companionway, in the bustle and confusion which seem to be indispensable in getting a vessel alongside a wharf, when it occurred to me to ask him at what hotel we were to stop. My venerable relative seemed somewhat taken aback at this question, cleared his throat nervously several times and finally informed me that, as a matter of fact, there were no hotels worth mentioning in St. John's, "though I believe," he added, "there are several establishments in the city dignified by that title."

I pondered a moment on this gruesome fact before inquiring, with sarcastic intention, where he intended staying. Should we have to pitch our tents in the streets, like this – squatters? My stepfather, who seemed anxious to avoid further controversy on the subject, discovered something demanding his instant and personal attention at that moment at the bow of the steamer and left me, muttering something of which I caught only the words "private boarding house" – "outside the city" and causing me to wonder dismally what manner of town was this which required no hotels and where the sole accommodation for the weary stranger consisted in private boarding houses outside the city. From this reverie Mr. Black's return aroused me. "Come!" he exclaimed, grasping my arm. He was a nervous man and always worked himself up into a state of great excitement when travelling. He assisted me forcibly down the gangway and across the wharf, fussily obtained a carriage, and we were soon progressing boarding-house-ward, seated in a vehicle which was considerably damaged by the lapse of time and drawn by a horse so extremely decrepit that I felt conscious of an apologetic frame of mind with regard to it and an inclination to alight and offer my services as a substitute.

This trip to Newfoundland, I may incidentally observe, was by no means a pleasure excursion as far as I was concerned, though I think my stepfather had no desire to preclude my deriving any enjoyment I could from it. Business in connection with certain mines in which he was interested had brought Mr. Black hither, and as he was not a strong man and required a good deal of attendance, besides suffering in an extraordinary degree from that malady incidental to most people who travel by sea, he thought that to have an agreeable young person constantly at hand to soothe his pillow, perform all sorts of little offices for him and look after him generally would be a very good idea. He unfolded this plan for my edification, assuring me that Newfoundland was a country well worth seeing and that such an opportunity might not occur again. After a good deal of persuasion, I yielded.

I remained in St. John's three months, during which time Mr. Black paid flying visits to contiguous out-harbours, and I was left very much to my own resources. I took long walks daily and saw everything there was to see in the town and its environments. St. John's is a unique little town, situated on a rugged bit of Atlantic coast, where it tumbles down one hill and struggles up another, the harbour intervening between the two elevations. The place is at once filthy and picturesque. Nature has done everything for it in the way of furnishing fine scenery, has surrounded it with rocks and hills whose grey tops assume a thousand fantastic outlines, and against whose base the sea comes surging up and pours into myriads of mysterious fissures and caverns with a thundering roar. With the natural advantages which it undoubtedly possesses, there is no reason why St. John's should not be a beautiful and flourishing city, except that it is not.

On some of the rocky hills that abound in the vicinity are forts, notably on Signal Hill, which stands at the northern entrance to the harbour and is what Byron would call a very sufficient mountain.[57] This formidable battery is garrisoned by one able-bodied person of four-score, a widower, who has sole command and whole charge of six most unmanageable pieces of ordnance. The town is very quiet in most parts, but there is always a certain bustle in Water Street and along the wharves, flanked by stores and tall warehouses and loaded with goods of various merchandise, here a cargo of hides, there a quintal of fish. Seamen are singing yee-hoing on board of sundry vessels lying at anchor in the harbour. In the spring, grinning sealers in oilskin suits are slouching about the quays or idling at the public houses in the vicinity. When they come back from their trip in a few weeks' time, they will bring with them so overpowering an odour that even the least fastidious passer-by will hesitate about venturing within a radius of a very considerable distance of their persons.

All trades here lie in most delightful confusion. Your grocer will probably display with pride a large and varied assortment of hats. In the dry goods shops you can buy anything "from a needle to an anchor," as they say here. At the apothecary's establishment you can invest in a miscellaneous assortment of wares – not forgetting a rope to hang yourself with if your stay in St. John's be very protracted. There are also a couple of bookshops where may be bought for double the usual price some periodicals, not more than three weeks old, from busier parts of the world.

The streets of St. John's are narrow, ragged and wind about in a tortuous manner, highly perplexing to the stranger, who loses his way frequently and brings himself up in the course of his wandering in quarters of unimaginable filth, tumble-down hovels, windows with broken sashes, decrepit fences, streets paved with old rags and decayed cats and other animals. One's nostrils are assailed by nauseating odours and one's eyes by loathsome sights and sounds. A more unsavory place cannot be imagined. One gets glimpses of dirty faces at dirty windows, ragged children, slipshod women, men with evil faces and slouching gait. But a glance into these regions is quite sufficient and robs one of any desire to penetrate farther. The town abounds in hills. I noticed that pedestrians, with few exceptions, walk even on level ground as though going uphill. This may possibly be accounted for by the fact that if you do go out it must be either up hill or down. I used occasionally to wish that the weary mortal might walk in any one given direction without either toiling up a hill or scrambling down one, but I do not remember that this wish was ever gratified. Mr. Black sometimes accompanied me in my peregrinations. On one occasion, I recollect, we went to town together and, to my inexpressible chagrin, were followed the entire length of Water Street by one or two street gamins with portions of their raiment on exhibition which should have been sacred from public scrutiny, requesting us to disburse to the extent of three ha'-pence. Mr. Black turned round to them now and then, menaced them with his stick and threatened them with the strong arm of the law, but this demonstration was ineffectual, and they continued their march, exhorting us meanwhile in tones of the last trump.

The town is entirely and shabbily built of wood, with the exception of a few of the public buildings. The striking-looking edifice on the high hill, whose towers are the first objects that meet the eye on entering the Narrows, is, of course, the Roman Catholic cathedral. It seems unnecessary to name it, as the Romans generally contrive to get all the best sites for building, even in Protestant colonies, within their own digits. Neither does the stranger need to be told that the grim, sanctimonious building on Cochrane Street, leading to the Allan wharf, is the Wesleyan chapel.

Newfoundland weather is uncertain. No man can speculate on it with impunity. A day beginning as though another deluge were at hand will clear up suddenly and for no particular reason, contrary to the glass and the prognostications of the weather prophets. The safest plan is never to contemplate a walk, even in the fairest and most promising weather, without arming one's self with umbrella and macintosh. The pedestrian may escape if he neglects this precaution, but the chances are that he will find both articles useful before his return.

St. John's rejoices in two newspaper organs, each claiming to be the voice of the people. The warfare between them is dire and unceasing. The *Telegram* refers to the *Mercury* as a polluted rag and alludes to its gifted proprietor as a "designing imbecile," while the *Mercury* retaliates by designating everything that appears in the rival as "drivelling slush."

The town likewise boasts one or two (so-called) concert halls around which hangs a forlorn air of gaiety, and which are occasionally peopled by itinerant theatrical troops of fourth-or fifth-rate merit from leading cities in the United States and the Dominion. The only play which I had the pleasure of witnessing during my stay in Newfoundand was *Hamlet* – very originally put on the stage. The star of the company was a man named Catesby – an ex-clergyman who had divested himself of his cloth and descended from the pulpit to the stage, where he had succeeded in acquiring the art of mouthing his words with exemplary skill. He fairly bayed forth his melancholy soliloquies. The appearance of the ghost did not accord with one's preconceived ideas of the orthodox stage spectre. He was clad in tights which were decidedly nonconformist – refusing to adapt themselves to the shape of the wearer. He was furthermore enveloped in a species of blue mosquito netting, the whole array forming a *tout ensemble* that was truly astonishing. As for the hapless young woman who played Ophelia, I really felt for her. Hamlet tossed her about the stage as though she were a doll, and when in their closing scene he advises her instantaneous retreat to a nunnery, he flung her from him with such force that she spun along the stage into the wings – where I sincerely hoped that someone was stationed in readiness to catch her, otherwise the consequences must have been disastrous.

I stumbled on some beautiful scenery in my various rambles. Anyone who forms his opinion of Newfoundland by what he sees of the coast *en passant* from the deck of his steamer receives quite an unjust impression of it. The grim, precipitous cliffs – with the surf of the broad Atlantic thundering against their base – than which nothing can be more uninviting, can give no suggestion of the exquisite loveliness of the scenery in the interior and on the western coast. The rugged heights, sombre, frowning, almost perpendicular in their grim monotony, are not without a beauty of their own, but nothing can surpass the silvery sheets of water, the soft undulating meadows clothed in tender green and the beautifully wooded grounds melting into ranges of hills, made blue by distance, that are to be found in many parts of Newfoundland. I found, not three miles from St. John's, moors – "barrens" the inhabitants of the country call them – wild, solitary, covered with short coarse grass and enclosed in a stunted growth of fir. Huge rocks, tumbled up, lay about, and the rushing of unseen waters alone broke the stillness. Here I was wont to sit hour after hour with my book, my solitude unbroken by sound or sight of living creature.

Near St. John's – so near as almost to form a part of the town – is the fishing village of Quidi Vidi (pronounced Kiddy Viddy), whose snow-white houses, fish flakes and rude fishing gear spread out on the rocks, coupled with the occasional view of a fisherman's daughter in orthodox red petticoat, form quite a fascinating spectacle when viewed from a distance. I use the expression "from a distance" advisedly. The enchantment of the scene vanishes as one approaches. It is not that the houses look less picturesque when viewed through a shorter distance of ether or that the fisher maiden's charms are not enhanced by closer inspection. It is simply that at some seasons of the year the odour disseminated by a Newfoundland fishing village is such, I do not hesitate to affirm, that the stink-pot used as a missile in war by the Chinese must be fragrant and balmy compared to it. Nevertheless, such was my curiosity that I walked through the village and out into the "gut" beyond.[58] I was much struck by the numerous cod flakes covered with split, soaked and salted cod spread out to dry. Under these structures, in some fishing stations the pedestrian may walk hundreds of yards completely roofed in by cod fish. But for the overpowering odour that permeates these structures one might glance at the water on one side sparkling through the boughs, and then at the roof whence only an occasional ray of light faintly glimmers, and imagine himself in the dingy streets, narrow and shaded, of some Oriental town. In any case, I suppose, one might hold one's nose and transport one's self there in fancy.

A large quantity of fish is exported from this place; I was told the exact number of quintals for this year, but I regret to say that I forgot it. However, it is just as well, for I have no intention of writing patent office records.

There are many beautiful little villages near the capital: Topsail, charmingly situated in Conception Bay, largely used as a summer resort by people who resign themselves to all manner of inconveniences, including exceedingly poor fare, to obtain the sea bathing. Here is a chance for some of our enterprising American cousins of a speculative turn of mind. A couple of good hotels, well managed, would make the place specially attractive and make also the fortune of the proprietor.

But the village, of all others, which impresses itself upon my memory is Portugal Cove. We drove there one balmy afternoon, and the first glimpse I got of it disclosed ragged cliffs stretching far out into the sea, with a group of huts situated, like the homes of some strange water fowl, in the very crevices of the rocks, far above the dashing white-capped waves and the roar of the breakers. At first glance these houses appeared inaccessible, but closer inspection revealed rickety ladders and steps cut in the solid rock. A dreamy, dismal place, I reflected, yet not without certain advantages as a residence. Gossip would be next to impossible because it would be a work of art to get from one house to another. But it is sad to think of the poor fishermen and women who drag out weary, lonely lives, and, dying in myriads, leave no records behind them to tell of their sorrowful, cheerless, hard-worked lives. On our way home we passed a beautiful sheet of water known as Twenty-Mile Pond. The size is expressed in the name. There it lay, not a ripple on its calm surface, glowing in the yellow sunset, surrounded by rugged hills – one of the magnificent lakes in which Newfoundland abounds.

After a sojourn of some three months in the capital, my stepfather appeared before me one morning with a face more flushed than usual, and surmounted by a hat very much on one side, his coat unbuttoned and the tails wildly flying behind him in the breeze, together with all other outward and visible signs of being in a hurry in his whole presence. Questions elicited the fact that he had just received a cablegram on business which necessitated his immediate departure for Tilt Cove, in the North, and that luckily the steamer was in port – would be leaving in an hour.

"Oh, Mr. Black," I implored, rising with tears in my eyes, "take me with you; do take me!"

"You? Why, wh–. It's no place for women. And, er – , you can't get ready in time."

"Try and see."

"Can you dress and pack your portmanteau and be ready to go down to the wharf in three-quarters of an hour? The landlady has to be interviewed too, you know."

"You try me, sir. If I'm not ready in time, I'll give you full permission to go without me."

"Very well. I'm afraid you will repent it. You're sure to be seasick. They tell me these coastal steamers roll terribly."

With this comforting information he left me.

15

Newfoundlanders on a Voyage from Boston in 1870

Samuel Greene Wheeler Benjamin (1837-1914) was born in Greece but educated in the United States, where he pursued careers as a journalist, author, and diplomat.

S.G.W. Benjamin, **"A Summer Trip to Newfoundland"**
Scribner's Monthly, 2 (1871): 618-25

Early in August 1870, I took passage in the little English Hermaphrodite brig *Clara* for St. John's, Newfoundland. It was a pleasant morning when we cast off from Long Wharf and dropped down the harbour before a light breeze, which gradually fanned the deeply laden craft outside of Boston Light. The wind freshened and everything promised fair until after nightfall, when the heavy curtain of gloom which overhung the land behind us, from whence issued the low growl of distant thunder and ominous flashes, indicated a severe storm travelling along the shore. It was evident after a while, from the increasing vividness of the lightening and the mist that was encircling us, that we were not to escape a touch of the storm. About midnight the wind struck us with the force of a heavy squall from the north; the storm was moving in a circle. We were now past Cape Cod, so the brig ran for an hour under easy sail before the gale, when, finding the wind likely to hold, Capt. Byrnes hove to under close-reefed foretopsail and fore and main staysails. The sea was rising fast, but the *Clara* rode like a duck, dry and easy on the seething waters, and about sunrise the force of the gale blew itself out. An observation at noon showed us to have been driven, by wind and currents combined, to the south of the "Georges" [Georges Bank]. All sail was now made, and I then had an opportunity to take a quiet survey of the ship's company.

All on board were natives of Newfoundland, excepting the captain, who was a native of Dublin, a Prussian before the mast – the best sailor on board – and the writer; and all, with three exceptions, were of Irish descent and good "Romans." I shared the diminutive cabin with four junk-dealers who had just disposed of a cargo of junk in Boston and were returning with an assorted cargo, part of which, a deck-load of apples, contributed towards making the brig roll hard and so overcrowded the deck that it was a ticklish operation passing fore and aft in bad weather to shorten sail, when blocks and sheets were snapping furiously and she was lying over to her scuppers. A young mechanic with his wife and another young woman completed the list of first-class passengers. To say that the accommodations were not what are usually found on American sailing vessels and that the fare was inferior to what is furnished to seamen in the forecastle of American ships is no exaggeration. Salt junk of the worst description and pilot-bread[59] highly seasoned of the kerosene oil and tar in the run formed our diet with a few potatoes, which soon gave out, and some tomatoes intended for the owner but served out to us in small rations as fast as they decayed.

The unfailing good humour of Capt. Byrnes, whose broad face presided benignantly at the table which he and the owner had conspired to furnish so meagrely, and the Attic salt and Irish wit of the junk-dealers were of some avail in covering the deficiencies of the *Clara's* lockers. Nothing could exceed the garrulousness of these worthy islanders except the everlasting chattering of a crowd of vociferating Arab donkey-drivers or the bedlamite tongues of Constantinople caïkdgees; and only the flashes of genuine humour and wit which enlivened their talk made their company endurable. Early and late they maintained the wordy Donnybrook, the endless discussions on questions suggested by their own experience regarding salvage, invoices, the rights of ships as carriers, quirks of marine law, the treatment of wives and the like – all stale and prosy enough but rendered novel by the animation, earnestness, dogmatism and occasional shrewdness displayed and the strongly marked individuality of the speakers. The debates were always spiced by the sallies of Johnnie Feene, who, though usually on the wrong side of an argument, often by a neat repartee threw unexpected confusion into the ranks of the opposition.

Amid a number of pithy statements which passed at random from one side to the other, two or three struck me as meaning more than perhaps the speakers themselves realized at the time. Said one of the disputants, "Aye, but remember, sur, that Newfoundland is two cinturies behind the times," a strange admission from an old sea-dog, and a Roman Catholic at that, who boasted elsewhere of the influence of Romanism on the island. Another said, "Maybe ye're right, but thin there's a great difference between justice and law"; so there is, my man, thought I, and bad luck to them that have wrought this divorce between right and intellectual might. A third, in reply to the observation "Shure, but ivery man defers to his own opinion," replied, "And of coorse, for ivery man's mind is a kingdom to him." Now here was a man who could not be accused of ever having read Percy's *Reliques*[60] or any extracts therefrom, giving utterance to this idea in words almost identical with the first line of the beautiful piece well known to all lovers of English poetry, "My mind to me a kingdom is."[61] The fact is that the same thoughts in similar language often occur to different minds without collusion, in different ages and countries; and what critics who have not studied their own or others' mental phrases choose to stigmatize as plagiarism is of much less frequent occurrence than they represent. Indeed, I am inclined to think that very often this charge is made simply that the critic may display his own acquaintance with the passage he cites, in proof of the charges so lightly adduced by his officious pen.

But if there was one topic more discussed by these junk philosophers than another, it was the supernatural. Bushnell[62] would have found them in full accord as to the reality of the supernatural and its relation to nature; and Robert Dale Owen's[63] *Footfalls on the Boundary of Another World* contains nothing more startling than the weird, mysterious yarns which were nightly told from actual personal experience in the little crowded cabin of the *Clara*: told, too, in earnest tone to listeners who heard with bated breath and, on occasion, corroborated the truth of the most impossible incidents. By attending with becoming gravity and an air of implicit faith, which, sooth to tell, almost turned sometimes into actual belief, I was permitted to hear the story of many a rare adventure or encounter with the powers of darkness. One of the narrators had fought an hour with the body of a deceased friend; another had been stopped on the public road to Waterford Bridge by a "sperrit" in the shape of a black dog; another had been within an ace of recovering hidden "threasure" from a foundered frigate, while a fourth had assisted in drawing "an irron chist of threasure" to the water's edge when the ghost of a man who was killed and buried with it to keep watch over it suddenly appeared and spirited it away, nevermore to be seen by mortal eye.

Johnnie Feene, of course, had his quota of marvels to relate, all of them sufficiently entertaining. One of his stories recounted the experience of a friend who, four years previously, had left his family starving at Bay of Bulls village and gone to St. John's in search of employment. Failing of this, he started for home and was met after nightfall by a black dog who addressed him and then, assuming human shape, informed him that he was an enchanted person fixed by a spell in a subterranean cavern near the Bay of Bulls and that his enchantment could only be abated by the entrance of someone sufficiently bold to brave the guardians of the cave and carry hence the riches it contained.

Overjoyed at the suggestion, the fisherman gladly volunteered to accompany the enchanted stranger, who accordingly introduced him to a subterranean hall, vast and gorgeous with oriental magnificence, where the wealth of the Indies lay apparently at his disposal, and he had it in his power not only to relieve the poverty of his condition but also to become the most opulent of Queen Victoria's subjects. But suddenly he was assailed by a troop of unwholesome ghouls who so disturbed his resolution that he fled to the upper air, renouncing possession of the riches in his grasp and leaving the enchanted man enchanted there forever.

Very naturally I was led to conclude that a more behaunted, bewitched and ghost-ridden country nowhere then existed than this same Newfoundland, which seemed to be an outlying station of Pandemonium,[64] as full of hidden treasures as the old haunts of Captain Kidd,[65] as beset with enchantments as the brain of Don Quixote,[66] as packed with ill-omened spirits as Alloway Kirk.[67] The imagination of these prosaic, storm-beaten old fishermen of Labrador teems with the feverish fancies of a nervous child; they are possessed by the fervid phantasies of the warm-blooded Southron.[68] The black dog figures in most of their legends and is evidently the bête noir of the Newfoundlandic imagination.

But all this time we were sailing towards our destination slowly but steadily. The dashing tide-rips indicated that we were on the Georges, "the graveyard of Cape Ann," as those shoals are rightly regarded, and the fishing schooners dotting the offing showed we were on the fishing grounds. It is very strange that no light-ship has ever been stationed on these dangerous shoals; many a ship must have met her fate on Cultivator's Ledge, where the depth is but three feet at mean low tide. It is not too late for the Government to put up a beacon there and thus mitigate the perils of one of the sailor's worst foes. A southwester took us towards Sable Island, but the currents seemed to combine with calms to set us nearer a direct line with that island than was comfortable. Somehow the brig failed to make the desired northing, and two successive observations did not allay the difficulty. It happened about this time that I took a trick at the helm. We were running with the wind a little abaft of the starboard quarter, and I noticed that the vessel, being too much by the stern and carrying too weather a helm from the pressure of her large mainsail, "griped," that is, had a tendency to fly into the wind, which rather aided in giving us a drift to the southward. On informing the captain of this he immediately took in the mainsail and gaff-topsail and kept the vessel away two points. The next observation indicated a very decided improvement in the ship's course, and on the following day we had the satisfaction of seeing in the southern horizon the low globular clouds called woolpacks, which in clear weather hang over the island and show where it lies when too distant to be visible.

Sable Island is the bugbear of the mariners coasting in its vicinity. It is so low that it cannot be descried until close at hand, is besides enveloped in dense fogs half the time and is so beset with swift tides and currents as to make it a very treacherous spot. Simply a sand bank scarce elevated above the ocean level, its sands are constantly shifting and altering its shape; so easily, in fact, are its sands blown to and fro that shipmasters who are wrecked there are recommended to make no effort to escape, as the sands will at once begin to gather around the grounded vessel and form a breakwater that will enable the crew to escape at their leisure. So soft and yielding is the beach that some years ago, on a quiet moonlight night, a vessel went ashore there so easily that none of the crew were aware when it was done; the watch were asleep, including the man at the wheel; the captain was in his bunk. And there she lay until daylight; then the master went on deck, and behold, his vessel was hopelessly aground on Sable Island! He afterwards received another ship but contrived to leave her ribs also bleaching on the same unlucky spot, and it is almost needless to say was not again entrusted with a command. The island is inhabited only by a corps of government wreckers, who communicate with the mainland once a month, and two or three hundred wild ponies bred from a stock wrecked there in colonial times.

From Sable Island we beat up abreast of Canso and made Scatari Light at the extreme eastern end of Cape Breton on the tenth evening. Louisburg, or what grass-covered mounds remain of that once famous fortress, lay hidden in the gloom to leeward, even its light being invisible. It was a black night and unpleasantly calm considering the proximity of the shore and that the tide was swinging us helplessly towards the rocks, against which we could hear more and more distinctly the deep rote of the long ocean swell. But about nine we heard a wind rushing over the water, which soon filled our sails and sent us plunging towards Cape Race, three hundred and fifty miles away; and a race indeed we had of it, running before a stiff breeze under all sail, rolling gunwhale under in the heavy following surges, the porpoises playing around the foaming bow with phosphorescent trail, and not rarely a huge whale starting up and spouting alongside. One fine morning a school of eight whales, good-sized fellows, passed close astern, remaining at the surface and tossing the smoke-like jets of spray into the air for some time.

Those who voyage in steamboats, while they gain in comforts suitable to an invalid, lose on the other hand much of the zest and flavor of sea life. Not for them is the adventurous sensation imparted to one who roughs it in a sailing vessel and enjoys the variety which comes with the observing of seamanship in the trimming of sails and the management of a ship in a blow, with the opportunity offered of occasionally turning to and lending a hand to haul on a halyard or brace or taking the wheel and associating on such germs of easy familiarity with the captain and crew as to relieve one of the feeling that he is a mere bundle of human merchandise transported for a given sum from one port to another with all possible dispatch – which is all very well for the man of business but is not pleasure. In addition to this, the constant grumble of a steamer's machinery prevents a full appreciation of the solemn grandeur of the ocean, deadening the wash of the waves and the sublime chant of the wind in the rigging. For the voyager on the sailing vessel is reserved that most weird of ocean sounds, the muttering and shrieking of Mother Cary's chickens [storm petrels] – those wandering gypsies of the sea, floating over the water through the gloom of a dark night like the eldritch laughter of lost spirits. Only on a sailing vessel can one realize in any degree what the navigators of other days have endured and imagine, as he tosses on the buffeting surges, that he is bound with the intrepid Vasco to discover the Indies, with Columbus seeks to evoke land from an unknown void, with Magalhaens is encircling the globe or with Raleigh or Sir Humphrey Gilbert is traversing the endless spaces of waves to discover Eldorado or quaff at the fountain of youth.

On the thirteenth day out we sighted Cape St. Mary's and stood all day along the southern coast of Newfoundland. Small fishing schooners were numerous, noticeable for their black sails, dyed in oil and tar to make them durable, which entirely ruins the picturesque appearance usual to fishing craft and aids to give a melancholy aspect to a shore that is already sufficiently barren and dismal. No other signs of life were visible from dawn until nightfall, except two or three fishing huts and the lighthouses on Cape Pine and Cape Race. Having a leading wind and no fog, we passed within half a mile of the latter, so famous for its shipwrecks. It is altogether a very cheerful spot, invested with the most agreeable associations. In Trepassey Bay, close at hand, two ocean steamers were lost quite recently, and just beyond, scarce a mile north of the cape, we passed the graveyard on the cliff where the remains are buried of those whose bodies were recovered by divers from the *Anglo-Saxon*, which struck while going at full speed in a fog and went down at the foot of the beetling crags. The *City of Philadelphia* was lost not far from the same spot, as well as many other ill-fated vessels. It may not be generally known that since the loss of the *City of Boston* the boats of the Inman Line have orders to give Cape Race a wider berth than heretofore, and it is to be wished that the change might be adopted by all the lines whose boats now shoot at full speed far too near that fog-enshrouded cape for the safety of the travelling public.

Under press of sail we glided up the eastern coast of the island, which welcomed us with a succession of chilling squalls from the high table-lands, which, with but one or two exceptions, is the formation of this part of Newfoundland. There was nothing inviting in the prospect. The rocky shore was like a huge wall falling sheer down most forbiddingly, seamed here and there by deep gulches, at the bottom of which two or three fishermen's huts might be discerned at long intervals. When we rounded Cape Spear, whose light is three hundred and seventy feet above the sea, the scene only became more grand and desolate. Before us towered Sugar Loaf like a stupendous bastion of Titanic mould, and the houses of St. John's were visible as through a telescope at the end of a deep gulch or channel, scarce a cable's length in width, guarded on either hand by perpendicular cliffs rising from five hundred and fifty to seven hundred feet, a tremendous spectacle. A wheezing, consequential little tug came out and towed us through the channel into the snuggest pocket of a harbor in the world and laid us alongside the wharf of the United States Consul, the owner of the brig.

St. John's is a place of about twenty-three thousand inhabitants; it is built on a slope and is a cross between an Irish and an English town and, except as it thereby represents an anomaly belonging rather to the Old than New World, offers nothing especially worthy of note to one who has been in Great Britain. The streets abound with dogs almost as if it were a Turkish city, generally of mongrel breeds, and burdened by a billet of wood hung to the neck, which renders them harmless. So numerous are dogs in the habited regions and so mischievous to the flocks that the laws of the island permit anyone to shoot them at sight. But while other curs are so common, individuals of the genuine Newfoundlandic stock are very scarce and always fetch from eighty to one hundred dollars. The breed is consequently guarded with great care but seems nevertheless to be dying out. No dog that is not entirely jet black and has not the web-foot and dew-claw is of the unmixed Newfoundland breed.

The port of St. John's is small but, as before observed, well sheltered and presents in summertime a bustling appearance, bring crowded with vessels of all nations. On entering the passage to the harbour a pungent "ancient fishy smell" informs the stranger what is the trade of the island. The energies of the islanders are devoted to the seal and cod fisheries. Early in March the seal hunters, as the sealing vessels are called, put to sea, cutting a way out through the ice if necessary, and strike directly for the ice fields in the Strait of Belle Isle, where the seals congregate in great numbers. From fifty to seventy-five men go in a sealer, their bunks being ranged gallery-like along the hold.

Half the proceeds go to the crew, half to the owner or planter; £30 is a fair average per man, £36 being occasionally made in one trip, and two trips are sometimes taken in the season, which lasts until May. The sealers are usually hermaphrodite brigs and are somewhat wedge-shaped in the floor so that when nipped by the ice, they are raised up instead of being crushed, slipping back into the water when the ice parts. Nevertheless, serious mishaps not rarely occur. Latterly, a few screw-steamers carrying 150 to 200 men have been introduced; their crews share only a third of the receipts, but the increased rapidity of locomotion enables them to gain equal profits with the other crews.

The best seals are those called whitecaps [white-coats], harps and hoods, the latter so named because the males, when attacked, protect their faces by a cartilagenous vizor, hard as India rubber and impenetrable to the spear. Two men are requisite to kill these – one to divert the attention of the seal while the other thrusts the lance through the throat. The men employed in this business wear snow spectacles formed of blue glass and protected on the sides by a fine network of wire, but even thus do not always escape a touch of snowblindness, which is very common and painfully acute.

The cod fisheries of Newfoundland are more profitable even than seal catching. Not only do her fishermen resort to the Banks, but all along the shore in her spacious bays they "till the farm that pays no fee,"[69] and the stages and flakes, or platforms for drying the fish, are to be seen at every hamlet, crossing above the street like vine trellises in Italy, bearing a fruit less fragrant and graceful but not less useful – codfish destined for the nourishment of good Catholics the world over, so long as Tuesdays and Fridays and Lent continue sacred to cod. It is interesting, when walking in the suburbs of St. John's of a pleasant day, to see the women and boys who cure the fish while the men are gone to sea driving carts into town from Quidy Widy

[Quidi Vidi], Empty Basket [Cove] and other little fishing ports, drawn by diminutive ponies and laden with salt fish ready to be shipped to distant lands. In other countries the peasantry flock to the shire town with vegetables and fruits, the product of the gardens and vineyards; in Newfoundland it is codfish that the peasantry carry to the market town.

And yet, although the profits of the seal and cod fisheries are large and all on the island are in some way connected with what is virtually its sole business, yet poverty of the most abject character is the rule among all but a very few. This business is under the control of monopolists and presents, by the way it is managed, an instructive example of what may result when the sense of mutual interest which should bind capital and labor is forgotten. Twelve men, most of whom reside in England and carry on the business through agents in Newfoundland, furnish the capital on which the fisheries are conducted; consequently a large portion of the profits does not remain in the country but is taken abroad to be distributed elsewhere. But this is a minor evil compared with the iron clutch by which these capitalists hold every fisherman, as it were, by the throat, scarcely permitting him to draw breath without their leave. The truck system,[70] so powerfully rebuked lately in Parliament and working disastrously in some of the Pennsylvania mines, is in full force in Newfoundland. The capitalists, in return for the fish, pay the fishermen in kind: that is, furnish them with all the supplies for supporting their families or carrying on their vocation, so managing as to oblige them to draw in advance of the profits of the still ungathered crops of fish or seals – a draft on the future – and contrive that the account shall always so stand as to leave the poor fisherman, already rendered improvident by this practice, always in debt and thus always in the power of the capitalist. In addition to this, the capitalists or their agents meet in a sort of club or Board of Trade room at stated periods and arrange among themselves the values to be placed on the supplies furnished to the fishermen in their employ, and from these prices, be they never so high, there is no appeal, nor, from the situation of affairs, is there any remedy to be provided against the repetition of the extortion. Gradually but surely has this tremendous tyranny gained strength on the island, and, so long as they remain under the present government, shuts all hope or power of improvement or progress in the condition of the islanders or the development of the mineral and agricultural resources which Newfoundland undoubtedly possesses in a large degree in its northern and western sections.

The island has nearly the superficial area of New England with a population of only a trifle over 150,000; and these, with the exception of St. John's and Harbor Grace, are doled out along the singularly indented and irregular coast in little settlements of half a dozen cabins widely separated from each other; and even this meager civilization is confined to the seaboard. Immediately on striking inland, one comes to the primeval forests of dwarf spruces, which are about as destitute of traces of the supreme Caucasian race as if Columbus had never been born. Half a century ago, one white man [William Epps Cormack] with an Indian guide crossed from the eastern to the western coast and wrote a valuable account of his trip and of the interior wilds; but no one has followed in his track, and the deer still migrate unmolested from north to south with the change of the seasons. The few Micmac Indians remaining live chiefly along the northern shore.

The Roman Catholics have, in former time, been in excess of the Protestants of the island and, as elsewhere, have characteristically secured the most commanding site in St. John's for their cathedral, which is the first object that meets the eye on entering the port, its imposing Italian architecture suggesting similar scenes in the Mediterranean and its size and position leading a stranger to infer that opulence and numbers are monopolized by the Romanists; but like all the Roman Catholic churches I have seen in the New World, the exterior is far more showy than the interior, which is cold and barn-like, finished off with crumbling stucco and poorly ornamented with cheap copies after the Masters: not an inapt symbol, methought, as I scanned its chilled walls, of the organization which it represents – to outward observers imposing and alluring but to those who inspect its internal system disappointing and repulsive.

The last census, however, showed that the Protestant element is gaining and is now in a respectable minority, chiefly of the Church of England but including a fair proportion of Scotch Presbyterians and Wesleyans. The Anglican Bishop of Newfoundland [Edward Feild] presides over the most extraordinary diocese in Christendom. The see may almost literally be termed the sea, for while it is the largest in limits in the world, it is almost entirely composed of water, and the good prelate discharges his episcopal duties by much traversing of the boisterous Atlantic. Newfoundland and the "vext Bermudas,"[71] with all the waters wide that roll between, are comprehended in this episcopate of many miles and few souls, unless we include soles that in the sea do dwell. A schooner-yacht is owned by His Reverence, who in the summer visits and confirms his northern flocks, a third of the coast of Newfoundland being thus circumnavigated by this ghostly yachtsman once a year; the fourth summer he rests from these maritime visitations, and the winters he devotes to the spiritual necessities of the Bermudas, who evidently receive more than their share of the spiritual nourishment. A suffragan bishop [James Kelly] resides at St. John's, and missionaries, as they may well be called, are set over the fishing hamlets. They take charge of several each and go from one to the other in fishing boats, faithfully and patiently doling out the scant store of religion to the poor islanders and, as one of their number observed to me, "endeavouring to make good Christians of them, or at least good churchmen."

It is supposed by many in the "States" that Newfoundland belongs to the New Dominion, while others, better informed as to that but, as would seem, against the best interests of our country, which already embraces all the territory we can take care of for the present, are endeavouring to create a movement in favor of the annexation of that island to the United States. For Newfoundland it would doubtless prove at least an advance on her condition as it is now, split by rival factions and under the control of monopolists who repress the energies of the people and prevent the natural growth of the multiform resources of the island. There are two political parties there, strongly divided on the question of confederation with the New Dominion, a measure which could only result to the ultimate advantage of the islanders. So it is properly regarded by the best citizens, but they are unfortunately still in a minority; and such is the ignorance of the masses that they are of course under the guidance of pestilent demagogues, those curses inevitably attendant on democracy in all ages who, for the accomplishment of their selfish ends, give currency to the most amazing stories against Canada, so incredible that we refrain from repeating them here, yet not too incredible for the credulity of those for whose benefit they are manufactured. The elections are attended by much excitement and corruption, and the intelligence and integrity of the legislature are not above suspicion. By annexing Newfoundland it is to be feared we should also annex a body of voters and pot-house politicians of a piece with the Tammany Sachems[72] and their horde "to vex Israel" and add another to the difficult problems which this nation is now trying to solve and digest, God only knows with what ultimate success.

There is some attempt at popular education on the part of the government, but judging from the intelligence of the popular mind, wisdom will not die with the Newfoundlanders. There is a reading room at St. John's, for the free use of which we here tender our grateful acknowledgements; but communication with the outside world is at best but scanty. The United States press is represented in the bookstores by the most vulgar of the New York weeklies, which may account for the not unreasonable opinion expressed to me by a usually well-informed clergyman that he supposed "the United States was entirely governed by mob law." The papers of St. John's are of a contemptible character; the telegraphic news they contain is much garbled, and what seems extraordinary, considering the near vicinity of Heart's Content, the terminus of the cable, is obtained via Boston and Halifax several days after date! Mail communication is maintained with Halifax, and the rest of the world thereby, twice a month by steam packet in summer but only once a month during the winter season owing to the ice; considering how rarely the mails have to be made up and distributed, the post office might almost seem a sinecure, and yet it will excite a smile to learn that the postal officials recently complained of overwork.

After all, we found it pleasant to be quiet a while and free from the turmoil and confusion, the constant hurry of events, the swift recurring rush of telegrams, the fever of life in the nineteenth century, and to live over a bit of "still life," as it was in some retired English seafaring town fifty years ago. And while one can hardly consider Newfoundland, with its pale sunlight and sere plains and infrequent mails altogether the place to live in, yet it is well worth a visit. Its aboriginal scenery, unexplored wastes, quaint capital, curious fishing ports, frowning coast, legendary lore, hospitable folk and blooming lassies with eyes of brimming blue, cheeks mantling with the roses of health, plump trim figures and elastic step, present a variety of attractions adapted to interest and please the stranger and store his memory with delightful recollections.

16

The Fire of 1892 and the Lure of Confederation

A.C. Winton was secretary of the Toronto Citizens' Committee formed for the relief of St. John's.

A.C. Winton, **"Newfoundland and Its Capital"**
Dominion Illustrated Monthly, 1 (1892): 657-66

The city of St. John's, the capital of Newfoundland and the scene of the recent terrible conflagration, lies upon the northern side of a splendid harbour, with a quick elevation at the rear of the city. This harbour forms a deep inlet on the extreme eastern coast of the island and is completely protected against gales from the Atlantic by two lofty ranges of hills. One of them, Signal Hill, towers almost perpendicularly 520 feet above the water, on the right of the very narrow entrance to the harbour. To the left of the entrance, South Side Hill attains to a still greater elevation. There is no city probably in North America more capable of defence and more impregnable than St. John's may be made. It requires no very great ingenuity to defend this Gibraltar of the western world.

The principal batteries are on the hills above mentioned, rising one above the other. These batteries were erected when the Island was threatened with invasion during the wars of American Independence and the French Revolution. Further in the entrance and on a steep cliff is situated the most powerful battery of all, called the "Queen's," containing bastions upon which guns may be mounted in full command of the entrance and harbour. The other forts of St. John's were situated upon elevated ground in the city about a mile apart – one at the south-east and the other at the north-west. One of them, Fort Townshend, still flourishes and forms the headquarters of the local police force. The other [Fort William] has been converted into the offices and station of the Terra Nova railway. The population of St. John's may now be estimated at between 30,000 and 40,000.

The event of the 8th of July last, when the press of this great Dominion announced that St. John's was totally destroyed by fire with a loss of nearly $20,000,000 worth of property, will ever be a memorable one to thousands of residents in Canada as well as to the stricken people of Newfoundland. The old disaster, that of the great conflagration in 1816, which repeated itself again in 1817 and again in 1846, seemed determined to complete the reduction of the city, rendering homeless thousands of its inhabitants. That day marked another dark period in the history of Newfoundland and will be remembered for generations to come as were its predecessors. With a good water supply obtained from an almost unlimited source and with considerable faith in the strength of their Fire Department, few in St. John's felt that the disaster of 1846 would ever be repeated. Such was the feeling of security that few people paid attention to the alarm of fire which sounded just before 5 o'clock on the afternoon of Friday, July 8th.

The weather had been extremely hot for some weeks, so much so, says the St. John's *Herald*, "that the grass had withered on the high lands and vegetation was everywhere dried up." Friday, the day of the fire, was one of the hottest days of the season: the thermometer had registered 87 in the shade nearly all the afternoon; at the same time a high wind prevailed. About 5 o'clock, the Central fire bell rang out an alarm, and in a few moments firemen were hurrying to the scene of the conflagration to find flames issuing from a stable at the junction of the so-called Freshwater and Pennywell Roads. Owing to repairs which were being effected in the main pipes, the water had been turned off, and before a supply could be obtained, the flames had made considerable headway, and as a stiff breeze was blowing at the time, the fire spread with incredible rapidity, leaping from house to house, with masses of burning wood and debris blowing hither and thither.

The fire began in a few short moments to assume grave proportions, and in less than an hour, the magnitude of the fire began to attract an immense throng of citizens from all parts of the city. Whilst one portion of the flames was rapidly spreading in the east, another was swiftly destroying the buildings in its course towards the south. Though the difficulty had about this time assumed a very serious character, no fears were entertained even then for the safety of the city generally, and it was believed the more substantial stone buildings would withstand the fury of the flames. Consequently, the English Cathedral and Gower Street Methodist Church were made the receptacles of large quantities of valuable property. At about 6.30 p.m. the magnificent Methodist College buildings were destroyed. This was followed by the destruction of the new Masonic Temple which crowned a rising eminence a short distance off. After this the fire raged furiously down several streets and quickly fastened on Gower Street Methodist Church, and in a very short while the parsonage was also in flames, together with the Orange Hall.

Meanwhile, flying masses of burning timber were scattered over the city, and in short time fires had started in several places.

Standing near the Synod Hall one could see a mass of flames rushing along and across the road, licking up the brick buildings in front of Victoria Hall. Presently it was seen that the Clergy House was on fire, and then the roof of the Synod Hall was caught. But a few yards off stood the English Cathedral, a gem of Gothic architecture and the masterpiece of Sir Gilbert Scott, and in a few moments the beautiful structure was a seething mass of flames. With a crash, heard above the din and noise of the elements, the roof fell in, and the result of the labours and offerings of generous people for many years vanished in a cloud of smoke. This building had been erected at a cost of not less than $500,000, the transepts and chancel having been lately added to the nave, which latter had been built forty years previously. Alas! It now stands a magnificent ruin. The fruits of half a century's labour, thrift and industry were destroyed in a few hours. Having worked its will upon the Cathedral, the fire now rushed to the group of buildings congregated together at the foot of Church Hill, and soon St. Andrew's Church and the Athenæum were in flames.

The Athenæum, which contained a library of many thousand volumes, with the offices of the Surveyor-General, the Government Engineer, the Superintendent of Fisheries and the Savings Bank was very soon in ruins. The Commercial Bank, not far distant, succumbed a few minutes later, and the telegraph offices had been consumed long before, the operators having to fly from their keys. Communication was thus cut off with the outside world. Consternation now seized the populace; they saw, with terror, that the stone buildings were no more able to resist the attacks of the fire than the flimsiest wooden structures.

As the night advanced, the fire swept up and down Water Street. A vigorous stand was made in one direction, which was effectual in stopping its progress west. The fire, which had taken possession also of the buildings in the northern part of the city, communicated to St. Patrick's Hall, and notwithstanding the great efforts made by the Christian Brothers and others, that fine building was soon in flames. It was then feared that the fire would spread to the convent and buildings on Military Road, the headquarters of the Roman Catholic denomination, but after a brave fight the danger was averted. A short distance lower down a collection of buildings also jeopardised the neighboring suburb, where numbers of those who had been previously burnt out had taken refuge, but with the assistance of many volunteers, the firemen and police succeeded, after severe exertion, in successfully combating the enemy.

Another severe struggle took place at the head of King's Road, where the security of a portion of Military Road depended on saving the Drill Shed, and already overtaxed energies were expended in fighting the flames. Citizens vied with each other in carrying pails of water to quench the flames. The fire had now reached down Cochrane Street, and it was hoped that the upper portion of this fine street might be saved. Attempts were made to pull down some of the buildings, but the effort proved futile until the fire had reached Hon. G.T. Rendell's[73] residence, the only house left standing on the east side of Cochrane Street. In the meantime, the waterside premises, stores, warehouses, wharves, etc., from Bowring's to Brooking's old premises, were a mass of ruins, including the stores of Hon. A. McKay, the tannery, Woods & Son's premises, Harvey's tobacco factory and bakery, the Coastal Steam Company's wharf and stores, and a portion of Hoyles' Town, with the Bavarian Brewery, W. Canning's and the American Consul's residences. Several vessels lying at the wharves had narrow escapes. The *Netley, Ethel* and others hauled out into the stream, although their sails and rigging caught fire several times. The steamer *Sharpshooter*, brig *Doore*, the coal hulk *Huntress* and a number of smaller craft were burned. By 5.30 a.m. on the 9th of July, the fire had completed its work of destruction. Fully three-fourths of the city lay in ruins, and $20,000,000 worth of property had been destroyed, covered by an insurance of only $4,800,000. Nearly 11,000 people were homeless and some 2,000 houses and stores destroyed.

When morning broke, the thick clouds of smoke still ascended from the burning ruins, and hours elapsed before it had cleared sufficiently to admit of a view of the tract of the desolating scourge. The misery of that awful night will long be borne in the memories of the witnesses, and the scenes of utter desolation and hopeless ruin, which became evident at every step, were sufficient to unman the strongest nerves and stoutest hearts. Of the immense shops and stores, which displayed such varied merchandise and valuable stocks gathered from all parts of the known world; of the happy homes of artizans and middle classes, where contentment and prosperity went hand in hand; of the comfortable houses where the laborer sought rest and refreshment; and of the costly and imposing structures and public buildings which were the pride and glory of its people, scarcely a vestige remained; and St. John's lay in the morning sun as a city despoiled of her beauty and choicest ornaments, presenting a picture of utter desolation and woe. On that fatal morning the populace gazed on the ruins and destruction of their homes, and then with the renewed vigor and buoyancy characteristic of Newfoundlanders everywhere at once turned attention to the difficult work of reconstruction and rebuilding their ruined city.

Kind hearts from Canada and other parts of the world at once generously came forward to tender relief, and to Canada belongs the glory of first coming to the rescue, and nobly did she do so. The first intelligence of the disaster reached Halifax late on Friday evening, July 8th, and His Worship the Mayor, who was informed of the calamity about midnight, immediately had notices inserted in the city newspapers on the following morning, calling a meeting of citizens at his office to take place at ten o'clock. At this meeting a committee was at once organized to purchase and forward to St. John's by steamer that evening supplies necessary for immediate relief, and in a few hours a fund of $4,000 was raised. Within a few days Halifax had contributed and forwarded to St. John's over $20,000 in money and provisions. Its example was soon followed by other cities and towns throughout the Province of Nova Scotia. The Provinces of New Brunswick and Prince Edward Island at once also organized committees of relief, and in a few hours generous help began to pour in from all the provinces of the Dominion to the people of Newfoundland.

The first intelligence of the disastrous conflagration reached Montreal on the morning of Saturday, 9th July, and an emergency meeting of the Council of the Board of Trade was called at once. A deputation was appointed to wait upon the City Council to urge the propriety and importance of a liberal grant in aid of their suffering fellow colonists; the deputation was most cordially received by the Mayor and Aldermen, and a sum of $10,000 was unanimously granted. At a public meeting of citizens at the rooms of the Board of Trade, and at which the Mayor presided, the following officers were appointed: Hon. James McShane, Mayor, Honorary Chairman; George Hague, Chairman; Chas. P. Herbert, Vice-Chairman; and later, the following Executive Committee was determined upon: Chas. P. Herbert, Chairman; Mr. Richard White, Treasurer; and Mr. Geo. Hadrill, Secretary. In a very short period the Committee had collected cash to the amount of $32,022.11 and in kind $7,549.87, making a total of $39,560.98.

Toronto, "the city of conventions and generous contributions," very appropriately named by a speaker in that city recently, also came forward with help. On July 13th a citizens' meeting was held for the purpose of devising some plan to aid the sufferers. The meeting was a very enthusiastic one and well attended. A list of headquarters was at once arranged in various portions of the city where clothing and provisions could be sent, and the following committee was appointed to carry on the work: A. Coyell, Rev. Father Ryan, Robt. Winton, Oliver Pooke, J.M. Ewing, E.E. Pike, ex-Alderman Phillips and Mr. A.C. Winton, Secretary. A sum of money was immediately placed in the hands of the committee, and with the assistance of the Board of Trade, a large sum was very soon at the disposal of the St. John's sufferers. Deputations were appointed to bring the matter before the City Council, when that body immediately granted a sum of $5,000. The Provincial Government also forwarded $10,000, and in a few days the generous people of Toronto had contributed, including the government grant, in money, provisions and clothing nearly $50,000. Deputations were also appointed to wait on the heads of the various denominations, and special collections were taken up in the various churches throughout the city, resulting in some thousands of dollars being forwarded to St. John's. Toronto truly did well and nobly.

From Quebec, Hamilton, London, Ottawa, Kingston and all over the Dominion, a generous and hearty collection was also made for the relief of the sufferers. It is needless to say how generously and willingly the call was answered. Citizens of all denominations came forward spontaneously to assist, and in a short while Canada was pouring in money, provisions and clothing to the distressed sufferers. Notwithstanding the somewhat hostile conditions which had recently embittered the relations between the Dominion and its sister province, all this was forgotten, and to quote the language of the St. John's *Herald*, "when our calamity came they forgot all this and nobly heaped coals of fire on our heads in vying with each other in their efforts to aid our fire-stricken city. All honor, then, to the noble-hearted and generous people of the Dominion."

Never did Canada do herself more honor than she exhibited in the generous and noble sacrifice she made to relieve her suffering fellow subjects in Newfoundland. All differences of opinion and all political issues seem to have been buried, and the people of this great Dominion seemed to vie with each other in affording relief. The value of this cannot be overestimated, and it has done more than anything else to deserve from the people of Newfoundland grateful thanks and to re-establish the old-time happy relationship between the two countries. The press of Newfoundland, representative of the various political views of the people, have acknowledged Canada's generous conduct, and the opponents there of confederation with Canada have had a good deal of their hostility removed. Everywhere throughout the island the feeling of sympathy and unity with Canada has increased, and the people of that island are now only waiting for a leader who will aid them in strengthening the ties of good fellowship and kindly feeling towards their generous neighbours.

That the question of confederation will be the most prominent plank of the next general election in Newfoundland there can be no doubt, and that the people are ripe for such a movement is acknowledged. After the election of 1869 the confederate party determined that they would not again raise the question until the constituencies required them to do so, and in no single instance since 1869, by word or act, have they made the subject of confederation a prominent feature of their party organization.

It is much to be hoped, now, that at the next general election there, this subject will be finally dealt with. A good deal, however, will depend upon the conclusions arrived at between the commissioners appointed on both sides to discuss terms of union. There can be no doubt whatever that the confederation of the island with the Dominion would be largely advantageous to both. We can supply Newfoundland with every article that enters into the daily consumption of her people, other than those she produces herself or may procure from the United Kingdom and which we cannot offer; whilst, in return for the advantage thus offered to our industries and agriculture, Newfoundland would be relieved of her financial obligations and receive her share of the general expenditure for all necessary internal improvements and would find a free entrance for all her exportable produce with the additional advantage of getting all her Canadian imports free of duty. Fiscally speaking, whilst the Dominion Government would make something by the transaction, the Canadian farmer, miller and mechanic would be largely benefited by it in the fact that all material now imported by the island from the United States could be better, more substantially and more cheaply supplied by Canada. This extension of her trade would be, in fact, the greatest advantage that Canada would derive from the union; but that means a good deal.

The question is frequently asked why the people of Newfoundland refused to enter the Dominion – a question that admits of several answers. The first is that Newfoundland had occasion to feel aggrieved at the fact that certain specific conclusions arrived at in her case at the Quebec Conference[74] were subsequently, if not repudiated, at least allowed to go into abeyance. Secondly, because her population, of entirely English, Scotch and Irish descent, whatever their local differences may be, are loyal to the core in regard to British connection and extremely suspicious of what, mistakenly perhaps, they regard as the laxity of a certain class of their Canadian fellow subjects in that respect. Added to this they had to contend with the influence of the commercial classes who were at that time – and are foolishly perhaps still – somewhat jealous of possible outside competition in what they are apt to consider as their own special preserves. The following opinion as expressed in the *North Star*, formerly published at St. John's by Mr. Robert Winton, gives perhaps a clear and concise view of some phases of the question:

"We believe – and we believe it honestly and sincerely – that our refusal to enter the Dominion is a matter of serious political and industrial embarrassment to us and that it may some day, not very far distant perhaps, involve us in serious commercial and political disaster. At present we are being ground to powder beneath the upper and the nether millstone. Our treaty relations with France, on the one hand, are annoying and offensive not only to our own government but to that of the United Kingdom, and the everlasting importunity of the United States government and its people are quite as intolerable as the other. Union with Canada would have enabled us to fight both issues on their merits – to cut off our relations with the latter entirely and to hold the former to the strict terms of the treaties. It is lamentable to reflect that the immunities and privileges which have so long been enjoyed by a few of our own people at the expense of all the rest, at the expense too of colonial and imperial patience, are still permitted to stand in the way of the only possible solution of our difficulties. Those who occupy that position have grave responsibilities to answer for, and it is time they should take these matters into serious consideration before they, too, are compelled to take their share of the common misfortune."

Since these prognostications were delivered every one of them has been realized in the financial and industrial relations of the province. The grip of France has been tightened, and the importunity of the United States has been persisted in, with much resulting commercial disadvantage. A few years ago, Newfoundland could enter the markets of the world upon an equal footing with the most favoured nation; today she is handicapped in the same markets by the bounty-fed produce [codfish] of France and the United States, taken from her own waters and disposed of at about one-half the price of her own. Her isolation has been otherwise very prejudicial to her interests and has seriously cramped her social and political improvement. It is to be hoped that she may ere long throw off her obstructive policy of isolation and take her place in the family of provinces to which she belongs. Her people are splendid examples of physical and intellectual manhood, hardy, cool, brave and industrious, accustomed for the most part to find their bread upon the waters[75] and to gather it with their lives in their hands. An intrepid race of men, such as they are, inhabiting that Gibraltar of America, would be a valuable acquisition to the maritime force of the Dominion and a valuable addition to its industrial and intellectual activity.

17

The Fire of 1892 (Poem)

Eros Wayback was the pen name of St. John's poet Edward St. George. Educated at St. Bonaventure's College, he became a teacher and before the arrival of the Christian Brothers was in charge of the Orphan Asylum.

Eros Wayback, **"The St. John's Fire of July, '92"**
Christmas Review, 1892, 8

The angel bells were chiming, on the terraced city's height,
All their bronze throats rhyming, of the advent of the night!
The sun's last rays were beaming, on Atlantic's restless flood;
Athwart his light was gleaming, where the sentinel city stood.

Harbored in its waters rode rich laden argosies;
Safe haven for those daughters, white-winged children
of the seas.
High th' anticipations, for this summer month of gold,
Quaffed be deep libations by the babbling brook or wold.

The angelus bells are ringing from yonder convent tower;
What bells, now, are flinging their harsh clangor to the hour!
Warning bells, these, mingling their clanging cries of fright
With silv'ry sounds just tingling on the fated city's height.

The fire-fiend rushes, roaring, irrepressible in might,
Swept boulevards and, soaring, shrouds high fanes in livid light.
Nought but desolation by the rising sun is seen;
The direst devastation where was joy but yester e'en.

Homeless thousands gazing on the ruins where their all
Moulders, fitful blazing, thro' that black and murky pall.
See but "In Memoriams" of the fire-fiend at whose nod
Razed were tall emporiums and the temples of their God!

18

Bringing Out the *Morning Despatch* After the Great Fire

H.W. LeMessurier
"How We Brought Out the Morning Despatch"
Christmas Review, 1892, 19

The great fire, which ceased on the morning of the 9th July, 1892, had destroyed the newspaper and printing offices of the *Herald, Telegram*, and *Colonist* – the three dailies – and of the *Times, Advocate, Royal Gazette* and Bowden's job office, so that no paper appeared on our streets that day, and everyone at eventide felt the want of the daily paper. Owing to the great and many changes of offices and business places, the want of some medium for advertising was felt, and, at the same time, citizens saw the need there was for the disseminating of news and the interchange of opinions regarding the unfortunate situation in which the city was placed. We made an attempt to fill the void, and, after a great struggle, were partly successful; and of the manner in which we had to accomplish it, I will try and tell my readers.

Saturday morning we held a consultation as to what means we should adopt to accomplish the publication of some sort of newspaper. One of our friends went to Harbour Grace to see if press or type could be there procured, and another went to investigate the resources of the city. Harbour Grace proved a failure, as no type or press was to be had in that city; but one of us hit on the *Patriot* office and thought we could manage to secure enough printing material there to fit us out, but, on sending an experienced compositor to view the stock, we were told that it was an impossibility to work off a paper from that office. So time passed until Tuesday, when the issue of the *Gazette*, on a 8 X 12 sheet, spurred us to a further visit to the *Patriot* office, which resulted in the conclusion of an arrangement with the owners for the type and Washington hand-press, which, for nearly half a century, had spasmodically worked off the never-dying *Patriot*. Notices were immediately bulletined around town that a daily paper, to be called the *Fire Fiend*, would be issued on the morrow, and as "ads" poured in, we prepared for the fray.

The *Patriot* office was in the basement of a house on the corner of Knight Street and Military Road, as dark and unwholesome a dungeon as ever a printer worked in. The type, which had been well worn in the service, was very much mixed, or, in printers' phraseology, it was in "pie" – if not all of it, certainly a great portion of it.[76] Some type was "standing," having remained undistributed for such a length of time that it needed nothing to keep it together, the old ink acting as a glue, and this required to be put in cases. Some type lay on the floor, scattered about, and but for the want of it would never have been picked up. Altogether it seemed like a forlorn hope to face this type and the "cases," to obtain sufficient material to publish a paper.

Our "comps" [compositors] looked in despair and muttered imprecations which nearly took the breath away. Twice, aye thrice, was the "stick" thrown down and a vow made that no more would we work at ungluing and scraping type and sorting "pie"; but at last we got enough together to set up some "ads" and a column of reading matter – in all, sufficient to fill one side of a sheet 11 X 16½. In the meantime, to make the office habitable, lime was procured, plentifully used, and the place swept up; but still the darkness was such that lamps had to be obtained and lit, even while it was day. This gave rise to a fear by the lady of the house above that a fire would be the result of using a lamp and a stove in such a place, and after much hubbub and the inspection of the place by a constable, we were once more in peace.

When we came to "make up" our paper, we were sadly short of leads, rules and other necessary furniture, and we discovered we had not enough large type to "set up" the heading, *Fire Fiend*; but we thought we could "set up" *Phœnix* and accordingly despatched someone to alter our notice from *Fire Fiend* to *Phœnix*, which had been hardly done than it was discovered that the type would not spell that classic name. There was P-E-N-I of one size of type, whilst the H and X were a size larger and could not be adjusted or made to look fairly decent. We were almost in despair, having tried "News," "Herald," and other names, when our "devil"[77] rooted out from the rubbish a wood-cut which read "The Morning Despatch" and reminded us of a short-lived journal which had one time been issued from the precincts of the *Patriot* office. We hailed the advent of that heading with joy and immediately set it in the "chase"[78] and "made up" to suit it. But what a time the "make-up" took, and what patient hard work there was, fitting leads and rules that were crooked or too short or too long and trying to make an adjustment of type which, although of one fount, was from different foundries and gave the patient compositors a fit of the blues.

On the morning of the 13th we launched our venture and readily sold eleven hundred copies which, as an advertising sheet, was gladly welcomed and as a souvenir of the fire was readily bought up. On the 14th we slightly enlarged our sheet and produced a 15½ X 19½ paper; but in doing so we exhausted all our available type and the "comps" struck work. The entrance to our office was by way of a yard, which was a veritable cesspool, and the stench from it "was enough to kill a dog," so we were informed by our factotum; and unless some other place could be obtained and better inducements held out to work, the *Despatch* was to die.

A consultation was forthwith held and an appeal made to the Hon. M. Monroe[79] for a spare room, who at once offered part of a store; and as a lot of second-hand type, kindly sent by the Halifax *Herald*, came to hand that day, we decided on shifting quarters. The type, which came from Halifax, was in its "cases" when packed in the case in Halifax; but when the package arrived here, the types were in "pie," and brevier, small pica and fancy advertising type were all mixed together. Everything seemed to go wrong, and the "comps" looked in despair. However, stands had to be made, type sorted and furniture procured, so each one set to work, and after a little delay we gave the public a four-paged sheet – each 13 X 9 – of solid matter and notified them that "the *Despatch* will, if possible, be published every morning."

Having second-hand type to deal with and being without the requisite quads, metal furniture for adjusting and "make-up," the make-shifts were often ingenious and curious. Our "chases" had been warped by the fire, and we could not get them straight. The type and the rules worked up, and sometimes the paper was issued blurred, cut, and looking as though it had the small-pox. Our "comps" were hard-worked in consequence of our having but enough type for one issue, and grumbling was the "order of the day." Several times we were in despair and almost concluded that the best thing we could do was to shut up shop; but we persevered and, notwithstanding that "comps" went and "comps" came, that the press gave out and the "ruby"[80] at times interfered with the working capabilities of some, we struggled on until the 24th of August, when our staff was drafted elsewhere, and the *Morning Despatch* closed down.

19

Problems Authenticating the 400th Anniversary of John Cabot's Arrival

Edward G. Porter was a New England writer.

Edward G. Porter, **"The Cabot Celebrations of 1897"**
New England Magazine, 17 (1898): 653-71

After four hundred years of unaccountable neglect, the discoverer of the North American continent has at last been himself discovered and crowned with something of the honor which is justly his due. How England could ever have forgotten him is one of those strange anomalies which are found sometimes in the history of any country. The real value of an achievement is not always apparent to the generation that witnesses it. The element of time must be allowed to show what results it has accomplished. But this does not altogether explain the treatment accorded to John Cabot; for time long ago revealed the vast indebtedness of England to his services. Yet no monument, statue or tablet has ever been erected to his memory until now.

There are, to be sure, some reasons to be given for this neglect. The voyages of 1497 and 1498 failed to bring any pecuniary returns, and the England of that day, like its thrifty king, saw little worth in lands discovered if they promised nothing in spices, gems or trade. Even the cod-fisheries did not attract the English as much as they did the Portuguese and French, whose hardy mariners resorted immediately, and in swarms, to the shores of Newfoundland.

The fact is the spirit of commercial enterprise had not yet been aroused in England. The home nest had not been shaken, and the bird of freedom and of conquest knew not how to spread his wings. Richard Eden,[81] in his *Decades of the New World*, published in 1555, reproaches England for not attempting more voyages to the west, as the Spaniards had done, for the conversion of the nations and for her own advantage, and "not ever like sheep to haunt one trade." "Cabot," he said, "touched only in the north corner and most barbarous part thereof, from whence he was repulsed with ice in the month of July. Nevertheless, the west and south parts of these regions have since been better searched by others."

This apathy of England was lamented also by George Beste,[82] who wrote in 1578 that the work was hindered by two causes: the lack of a generous nobility and the want of skill in cosmography and the art of navigation. These causes were destined, however, to be soon removed and the "navigation which in the time of Henry VII was very raw" grew in the brilliant reign of Elizabeth to magnificent proportions.

This remarkable change was reflected in the literature of the country. No notice of Cabot's exploit was taken at the time; and, incredible as it seems, there was no printed account of it in the English language for fifty-eight years! And yet Peter Martyr[83] published a narrative of it in Spain in 1516 and Ramusio[84] in Italy somewhat later. But when the great sea-rovers started out from the west of England ports and led the way to colonization, English writers were no longer silent. Entertaining descriptions of the voyages followed in rapid succession from Eden and Gilbert and Churchyard and Stowe and Hakluyt and Haies and

Peckham, enlightening and stimulating the people as to the wonders of the new land beyond the sea.

The merchants now came to the front and seized the opportunity with a degree of energy and zeal never before witnessed. They were too busy with their schemes of adventure in 1597 to trouble themselves about the men who had opened a path for them across the Atlantic in the days of their grandfathers – if indeed there was anywhere in the world at that time such a thought as a celebration of anything.

Besides there was always confusion as to the person entitled to the honour of the great discovery. No one stood out clear and foremost as Columbus had done in the South. It was "The Cabots" or "Sebastian Cabot and his father" who divided the honours; and for a long time neither of them seemed of any account. The father had died, no one knew when, where or how; and the son passed into obscurity for fourteen years, when he emerged in Spain under royal favor, first as naval captain and then as pilot-major, a position of distinction and emolument, which he enjoyed through the greater part of his life. This gave him the opportunity in the preparation of charts or in conversation with his friends to state things as he chose in regard to the voyages which he claimed to have made, either alone or with his father, and his word was generally, though not always, accepted.

The result has been that, with Sebastian as the only informant, the two voyages became hopelessly mixed in the public mind, and Sebastian has had all the glory. His portrait, too, has served to keep alive his assumptions, while his poor father rested in oblivion. All the writers until recently made obeisance to the son. It is rather surprising indeed that no monument has been erected anywhere in his honour. We may congratulate ourselves in this country that the suggestion of William Doyle in 1770 to name North America "Sebastia" did not take effect. If it had, we should have been saddled with a far greater historical inaccuracy than is now the case with "America," which in the judgement of many is not so far wrong after all; and the name is really an ideal one in itself. "Cabotia," which was advocated at one time, would have been correct as applied to North America, with the understanding that it commemorates the father.

All these errors might have been avoided if the papers, chart and globe of the elder Cabot had not mysteriously, and, as many believed, surreptitiously disappeared on his return from his first voyage. And we should have known much more of the truth if any proper attention had been paid to the letters patent which were published by Hakluyt[85] in his *Divers Voyages* in 1582, showing clearly to whom the grant was made. Hakluyt also tells us that Sebastian's maps and discourses were then in the custody of one of Cabot's old associates, William Worthington, who was willing to have them seen and published. But apparently they never were seen and published, and what became of them no one knows. William Worthington therefore becomes, like Sebastian himself and the Spanish ambassador, a suspicious character.

And so it has come to pass that we have not a scrap of information about either of the Cabots in their own handwriting; and in the general confusion, we are left with only what others have said and written about them – and that almost exclusively about Sebastian. Until lately no one has attempted to reconcile the glaring discrepancies in various accounts. Each author has followed the errors of his predecessors and transmitted an ever-increasing bundle of unproven, contradictory and vexatious statements, and these have composed the materials of the Cabotian history.

Happily, however, for the cause of truth, after three centuries and a half of groping in the dark, the modern critical demand for original documents has led to a thorough and costly search among the great archives of Europe. This effort has been rewarded by the discovery of certain writings of exceeding value. Those which bear directly upon our subject may be enumerated here for the convenience of the general reader, especially as they have formed the chief topic of discussion at the recent celebrations.

Original Documents Bearing on the Cabot Voyages

1. The naturalization papers granted to John Cabot by the Venetian Senate, 1476, in consideration of a residence of fifteen years.
2. The Letters Patent issued by Henry VII, March 5, 1496, to John Cabot and his three sons, Lewis, Sebastian and Sanctus, with authority to visit under the royal banners all the countries and seas of the east, of the west and of the north. The south was prudently omitted in this broad licence.
3. The entry in the Privy Purse expenses, August 10, 1497, of a gratuity of £10 "to hym that founde the new Isle."
4. A private letter from Lorenzo Pasqualigo to his brothers in Venice, dated London, August 23, 1497.
5. An official despatch written the very next day by Raimondo de Soncino, envoy of the Duke of Milan in England.
6. Another communication from Soncino to his government, dated the following December.

The last three documents all refer to the first voyage and show that North America was discovered by John Cabot in 1497. They do not mention the name of Sebastian.

7. Memorandum of a pension of £20 per annum, granted by Henry VII to John Cabot, dated December 13, 1497. A charge upon the customs of the Port of Bristol.
8. New Letters Patent issued February 3, 1498, to John Cabot. No mention is made of his sons.

9. Memorandum of loans from Henry VII to some of Cabot's companions "going to the newe ils."
10. Despatches sent to Ferdinand and Isabella by De Puebla and De Ayala, Spanish ambassadors in England, referring to Cabot's map and describing the departure of the second expedition.
11. La Cosa's celebrated chart of 1500.
12. The *mappemonde* of 1544, attributed to Sebastian Cabot.

These are substantially all the contemporary documents thus far brought to light. They have cleared many doubts and established a few very important facts which the writers of our time have eagerly improved. It was fortunate, indeed, that these new materials could be given to the world and examined before the completion of the fourth century of the great discovery. Otherwise we should hardly have known what to celebrate, when to meet, whom to honour or how to distinguish the two voyages.

The main facts to be kept in mind are that John Cabot was a Genoese and his wife a Venetian. They lived in Venice many years and had three sons. He made voyages to Mecca, Portugal and Spain. About 1490 he settled in England with his family and was known as an experienced seaman. For several years he entertained the idea of crossing the ocean. Under royal authority he commanded the *Matthew*, sailing from Bristol early in May, 1497, with a crew of eighteen men, nearly all of whom were Englishmen.

John Cabot landed on the North American shore in June 1497 and planted there the banner of St. George and the winged lion of St. Mark. He coasted for several days, finding "an excellent and temperate climate" and making no mention of ice. He saw no human beings on that voyage but found signs of occupation in felled trees, snares for game and a bone needle for making nets, which he brought back for the king. He was again in London on the tenth of August, having accomplished the whole voyage in about three months.

Some of the questions still unanswered may also be stated:

1. When the Cabot family became residents of Bristol and where they lived.
2. As to the date of the landfall, whether June 24, as is commonly believed, or a week or two earlier, as suggested by Harrisse.[86]
3. As to the place of the landfall – a question of great interest. This is warmly contested, there being no documentary evidence until 1843, when the so-called Cabot *mappemonde* was discovered, locating the *Prima tierra vista* near the northern part of Cape Breton.
4. As to the statement in Pasqualigo's letter that Cabot "coasted 300 leagues."
5. What the two islands were which he saw to starboard on his return.
6. When and where John Cabot died and under what circumstances.
7. The burial-place of either John or Sebastian.
8. Where and when Sebastian was born.
9. Whether Sebastian accompanied his father on the first voyage, or even on the second.
10. When the second expedition returned and what was said of it.

With this revived interest in the study of the Cabots it was inevitable that so great an event in human history as the finding of this continent could not pass another centennial period without being noticed. Events of far less importance are being commemorated every year in all civilized countries. The echoes of the Columbian pageants in Spain and Chicago were still in the air; and although British subjects have never disputed the just claims of the great admiral, they have learned in these latter days to recognize the debt they owe to that other Genoese, who added more territory and more wealth to the crown of England and to the English-speaking race than any other man.

It is interesting to notice that the first proposal for the observance of Cabot's quadri-centenary came from Newfoundland, England's oldest colony. The Rev. Moses Harvey, the esteemed historian of that island, published a communication in the *Maritime Monthly Magazine* as far back as 1874,[87] advocating such a celebration; and the Royal Society of Canada must be credited with being the first organization to take the matter up energetically, guided by the enthusiastic efforts of Dr. Bourinot.[88]

A deputation of well-known Canadians went to England in June 1896 to recommend an appropriate commemoration there. They were hospitably entertained at Bristol at a dinner given by the Mayor and Mayoress, and the suggestion that some monument to Cabot be erected in Bristol, simultaneously with one in Canada, met with warm approval. A large committee was appointed to obtain ancient documents, charters, portraits and other relics illustrating the naval enterprise of Bristol in the fifteenth and sixteenth centuries and also to arrange for some worthy memorial in the form of a statue "of one or other of the Cabots," or of a group, to be inaugurated on the anniversary in 1897. At the same dinner, the United States Consul, L.A. Lathrop, Esq., expressed his hearty interest in the movement and only regretted that his own countrymen did not seem to recognize the full importance of the event which pre-empted the North American continent for the Anglo-Saxon race.

The plan of a memorial tower met with general favor, especially as Bristol had a magnificent site for it on Brandon Hill, a lofty and conspicuous elevation, with twenty-five acres of unoccupied land, considered to be "the finest inter-urban hill in England." It has the great advantage of being equally accessible to the old city and to the popular modern suburb of Clifton. The exquisite panoramic view embraces the English and Welsh hills, with the broad, sparkling waters of the Bristol Channel lying between and the meandering Avon threading its way through the heart of the city and then disappearing under the neighboring cliffs till it hastens to join the great estuary at Avonmouth, where the new docks afford ample facilities for the reviving trade of Bristol with Boston and other transatlantic ports. On the top of Brandon Hill there was once an old hermit's cell with a chapel dedicated to St. Bernard, who came hither with his Irish mariners after their traditional wanderings over the "Sea of Darkness." The spot thus acquired sanctity in the eyes of all sailors, and it was their custom in Cabot's time to visit the old shrine before embarking on their voyage, and again upon their return.

The tower which is to occupy this commanding situation is an ornate example of medieval architecture, such as can occasionally be seen in France and Italy. It has continuous buttresses at the angles from base to summit. The upper story will be relieved by ornamental balconies. Panels are provided near the base for bas-reliefs and inscriptions, one of which will be filled in by the American subscribers.

The corner-stone was laid by the Marquis of Dufferin and Ava with imposing ceremonies on the 24th of June 1897. It was fitting that this honorable service should be entrusted to a former Governor-General of Canada and one familiar with nautical achievements as the author of *Letters from High Latitudes* is known to be. Of course the eminent guest received the official presentation of the freedom of the city, according to the ancient usage.

In opening his address Lord Dufferin complimented Bristol upon her desire to honor the man to whom England is indebted for two of the most precious jewels in her crown – Canada and

Newfoundland. Bristol men were founders of England's power on the high seas. It was the encouragement they gave John Cabot that induced Englishmen a little later to follow the sea as a profession. The speaker then dwelt upon the old beliefs in the existence of mysterious lands beyond the setting sun that haunted the imagination of Europe so long. Geographical science was at a low ebb when the map-makers were so stuffed with travellers' tales that they delineated chiefly a population of dragons, griffins, mermaids, unicorns and other monsters until their charts resembled a zoological museum. The Arabs preserved more correct notions, but they always had a horror of the Western Sea and declared that anyone attempting to invade its waters should be considered insane and should be deprived of his property and all civil rights.

Cabot appeared upon the scene just as Bristol had been fitting out expeditions, year after year, in search of those elusive isles which were on all the maps of the time. We can imagine him setting sail that May morning with his crew on the *Matthew*, with its lofty poop, low waist and plunging bow, and "after what must have been a prosperous voyage sighting the Cape of Bona Vista, or whatever point on the coast of Newfoundland, Labrador or Cape Breton the learned may determine to be his landfall." The results flowing from Cabot's northern expedition were infinitely superior to those which followed the Spanish conquests and colonizations. The Spanish adventurers brought vast regions under the dominion of the Spanish crown and for a time poured rivers of gold into the Spanish treasury; but they inaugurated a barren policy of cruelty, rapine and extortion, which led to the extinction of two interesting and original civilizations, to the demoralization of the conquerors and eventually to the impoverishment of the kingdom whose revenues had been thus artificially inflated.

On the other hand, John Cabot, with the intuition of genius, acquired for us a permanent footing in a vast territory peculiarly fitted for the development of the best forms of human energy. Instead of cities, temples, palaces and rich cultivated lands, he found desolate primeval woods, ice-bound rivers and a bitter climate. And yet it was amid such surroundings that he hit upon a mine of wealth richer, more perennial and more stimulating than the El Dorados of Peru or the ingots of Mexico.

Alluding to the wise colonization policy of Raleigh and Bacon, Lord Dufferin spoke of the "virile and austere Protestant settlements of New England," which carried with them the germs of that republican spirit which has found its expression in the numerous and mighty commonwealths which now constitute the United States. The initial step in this prodigious spectacle of human progression was taken by John Cabot, who opened the door for us to the great continent. How different the moral lesson in the case of Columbus, in whose caravels "lurked the Inquisition, slavery, the carnage of Cortez and Pizarro, the devastating policy of viceroys and a permanent instability of affairs."

While these exercises were going on at Bristol, congratulatory cable despatches were exchanged with the Royal Society of Canada, whose proceedings at Halifax were attended by a numerous company from different parts of the Dominion, together with invited guests representing some of the older universities and historical societies of the United States. The meetings continued through the greater part of the week and included a brilliant series of festivities, notably those of the 22nd of June in honor of Her Majesty's Jubilee. The Province building was placed at the disposal of the Royal Society by the government of Nova Scotia.

Among the papers read before the historical section were three which deserve to be mentioned. One was by the Hon. John Boyd Thatcher, Mayor of Albany, who in a graphic style portrayed the first voyage, following the very meagre accounts which are left to us and outlining the probable course which according to the speaker's measurement must have led Cabot to a landfall far up on the Labrador coast. The second voyage was also considered. Mr. Thatcher exhibited some interesting relics from his private collection. Among them was a large and well preserved autograph letter of Henry VII, which we are permitted to reproduce, on a smaller scale, with this article. It is written not in "King's English" but in "royal" French and with slight regard to grammatical accuracy, as we should deem it today. The letter appears from its contents to have been written in 1506. Philip and Joanna had just visited Henry at Windsor, on their journey to Spain to assume the sovereignty of Castile. Philip's relations with Ferdinand were somewhat strained, but this letter shows the warm place he had won in Henry's heart. Although the document does not technically belong to the Cabot literature, it sheds light upon some features of the character of Cabot's king, and therefore it belongs to the period which we are considering.

Another interesting Cabot paper was given by Dr. S.E. Dawson of Ottawa, whose elaborate treatise on the subject in 1894 was printed in the *Transactions of the Royal Society* and received with much favor,[89] though naturally with some criticism by those who oppose the theory of a landfall at Cape Breton. In fairness to his opponents, Dr. Dawson summed up the whole question in a clear and scholarly manner, answering in detail the objections that had appeared from any quarter and seeking to dispel the traditional misconceptions which had so long overlaid the subject. His careful study of the contemporary documents and of topographical and climatic conditions gave emphasis to his conclusions, which, it must be said, carried conviction to many of those who heard him.

In all the discussion at Halifax, each of the two voyages was considered wholly by itself. The old mystification which arose from confusing the two and treating them as if they were one has been a hard incubus to shake off from the public mind. Although

Sebastian Cabot, that "Sphinx of American history," was himself largely responsible for this and for many other serious blunders, he has not been handled as roughly in America as he has by some European writers. He is regarded here as a man belonging to his time, not an "unmitigated charlatan" but diplomatic, self-seeking, unfilial, treacherous and apparently sometimes untruthful. But all this may be said of the kings and courtiers and ambassadors of that day; and we must always remember that we have no writings extant from Sebastian himself about any of the matters in controversy. If he were now in court, he might be able to justify himself on many points; perhaps not, but we may at least give him the benefit of the doubt.

The president of the Royal Society, Archbishop O'Brien,[90] read an elaborate and ingenious paper, illustrated by diagrams, showing from the *mappemonde* that the landfall might have been southwest of Cape North, within the Gulf, and that the island of St. John would then have been Prince Edward Island. Taking up the La Cosa chart, he gave an explanation of the meaning of Tanais in Soncino's despatch which confirmed his position. He then sought to discover the scale of Cabot's shoreline on Cosa's map, and by a skilful process of reasoning he obtained three-eighths of an inch to a degree. Thus equipped, the president felt authorized to claim that *Cavo d'Ynglaterra* is Cape Chidley and *Cavo de Jorge* Cape Race. Other points are identified, and the chart, he thinks, extends from Cape Henry to Hudson Straits.

A poem on Cabot was ready by Mr. W. Wilfred Campbell.[91] Among the guests of the Royal Society the place of honor was justly given to the delegates from Bristol, William Robert Barker, J.P., and William Howell Davies, J.P., both being ex-mayors of that city. These gentlemen were warmly applauded whenever they spoke, and by their presence and their enthusiastic addresses they added much to the dignity and significance of the occasion.

The chief object of the meeting at Halifax was to erect in the

Province building a large and elegant bronze tablet to the memory of John Cabot. The ceremony took place on the 24th of June, in the presence of a large assembly, including the Governor-General of Canada and Lady Aberdeen, Lieutenant-Governor Daly of Nova Scotia, officers of the army and navy, U.S. Consul-General Ingraham, the Consul-General of Italy and representatives from various parts of the Dominion and the United States.

The Earl of Aberdeen unveiled the tablet with characteristic felicity of manner and of speech. He paid appropriate homage to the grand old sailor and said it was only after the labor of all these centuries that we have been able to understand the importance of his discovery.

A picturesque incident occurred at the close of the ceremony. A group of Micmac Indians, men and women, appeared upon the scene, dressed in the brilliant gala costumes of their tribe, and came forward to present gifts of their own handiwork to the countess, who received them in a very spirited and gracious manner. The thought that these children of the forest were descended from the people whom Cabot found on these shores made their appearance the occasion of a spontaneous and long-continued outburst of applause.

It will be noticed that the inscription on the Halifax tablet does not commit the Royal Society of Canada to any particular theory of the landfall. Most if not all of its members now accept Cape Breton Island, though unable as yet to agree upon the exact spot; but in common with all other scholars they allow that, wherever Cabot may have first sighted land, he certainly visited Newfoundland and explored much of its coast. The residents of that oldest of England's colonies are justified in making much of their inheritance in the name and fame of the great discoverer of the North. Some of their writers, like Dr. Harvey, accept the Cape Breton hypothesis. Others, like Judge Prowse and Bishop Howley, hold tenaciously to Bona Vista or Cape St. John. The debate is likely to be continued, if for no other reason, out of local pride. But no one will grudge the plucky Newfoundlanders their right to appropriate as much of Cabot as they please. If the latest learning does not sustain their cherished traditions, they may say in reply that they are still prepared to argue the case. They may affirm that they do not accept the *Mappemonde* because it rudely disturbs the belief of ages; and as for the Cosa chart, it is a mere crude sketch and may be made to prove anything. It is based, they claim, on very imperfect information, obtained perhaps from some sailor carrying fish from Bristol to Malaga.

Meanwhile Newfoundland makes no mistake when it celebrates the arrival of the good ship *Matthew*, that noble forerunner of the fleets that have since sought her harbors and drawn untold wealth from her Banks. It was a brilliant scene, witnessed last June in the enterprising city of St. John's, when the gathering processions of official dignitaries, military and naval officers, clergy, merchants, civic bodies, industrial clubs, temperance and Masonic orders, school children, fire brigades, united fishermen and other organizations were wending their way, with music and banners, through the decorated streets to the broad carriage-road leading to Signal Hill. This is the summit of a mountain ridge twice as high as Brandon Hill at Bristol. It rises sharply on the northern side of the entrance to St. John's harbor and is said to be the most conspicuous landmark in any city in America.

Here in the presence of thousands of citizens was laid with due formalities the corner-stone of the Cabot Signal Tower, a massive structure to be built of rock quarried on the spot. There are two veins, purple and blue, which will be used alternately. The square, two-story central hall is flanked by square, castellated towers, one for a signal station and the other for an observatory. The lower story is to have thick battering walls, the roof will be battlemented and the flanking towers armed with bastion lookouts. The pedestal tower suggests the Palazzo Vecchio at Florence. Signal Hill was formerly imperial property and was occupied by a garrison. The old-block-house may still be seen. The time is still given to the city by the firing of a gun here at noonday – the only specimen left of the many saucy muzzles with which the hill once bristled. The presence of several warships in the harbor bearing the British, French and United States flags and decked in the fullest holiday bunting added much to the gala character of the day.

* * *

The principal addresses made on this occasion were by His Excellency the Governor, Bishop M.F. Howley and the Rev. Moses Harvey, LL.D. One of the best poems of the Cabot centenary was written by Sir Robert Thorburn of St. John's.[92] The Newfoundland government issued a series of beautiful postage stamps illustrating Cabot, the Queen's Jubilee and the resources and sports of the island, such as fishing, sealing, mining, logging, caribou and ptarmigan hunting and views of scenery.

If the Eskimos, of whom Lieutenant Peary has been telling us so much lately, had only attained a higher degree of civilization, they would no doubt be on hand in these days ready to prove their claims and to set up a memorial to Cabot on their rock-bound coast, somewhere near latitude 60 degrees. They have not yet been heard from in connection with the celebrations of last summer. But their cause is not left without a champion, and that, too, one of the knightly plume in the contest – even the foremost scholar in Cabotian research, to whom all other writers are confessedly indebted, whether they accept all his conclusions or not. The name of Harrisse[93] carries great weight, but as his Labrador theory is drawn from statements which are capable of other interpretations without violating the local conditions of the problem, he is not generally followed by our western writers, who find his position in this matter untenable.

It should be said that the Maine Historical Society observed the Cabot festival, at its meeting in Brunswick, by a series of valuable papers covering the main aspects of the subject, read by the president, Hon. J.P. Baxter, and several other members of the society.

This paper would not be complete without a reference to the fine Cabot group exhibited last summer at the New Gallery, London, by John Cassidy of the Manchester Academy of Fine Arts. This young Irish artist has received many proofs of his talent in the shape of prizes and medals and high commendation from the critics. His orders for statues have followed in rapid succession, and he has just executed one of the Queen in colossal size for the city of Belfast. This group of the Cabots will bear close inspection, and it is sure to increase the fame of the artist. So far as is known, this is the first attempt to represent either of the Cabots in the plastic art. One could wish that it might find its way to this country. It would be a great acquisition for any of our museums, libraries or clubs.

The festival celebrations of last summer were not expected to add original materials to Cabotian literature. Such materials were brought to light a few years ago and have been already described in this article. But the celebrations have done much in calling attention to the results of the latest scholarship and in restating both the facts and the theories. The occasion has also brought out a few new books, like those of Weare[94] and Beazley.[95]

The year has indeed given us one ancient record relating to Cabot from a contemporary roll hitherto unknown. It was found early in 1897 by Mr. Scott of the British Museum, whose researches in the Westminster Chapter House muniments were rewarded by the discovery of the following item referring to the pension money collected for Cabot: (No. 12,243) endorsed,

"Brystolle, the Accompts of the Custymers." Entry No. 2. *"Bristolle Arthurus Kemys and Ricardus A. Meryk Collectors Custumarum et Subsidiorum Regis ibidem a festo Sancti Michaelis Archangeli anno tredecimo Regis nunc usque idem festum Sancti Michaelis tunc proximo sequens reddunt computum de £1,126 7s. 10d. Etiam in thesauro in una tallia pro Johanne Caboot £20."*

The name of Cabot has had a variety of spellings. The writer has encountered no less than sixteen different ways, some of which would hardly suggest the great navigator at all. There is no known connection between these Italian Cabots and the Huguenot Cabots of the Channel Islands. The representatives of the name in this country are descended from the latter.

In conclusion, a caveat must be entered against the error contained in the *mappemonde* which gives 1494 as the date of Cabot's discovery. The origin of this blunder has been sufficiently explained; but respectable authors like Tarducci, H.D. Traill in *Social England*, vol. II, and Sir Walter Besant in *The Rise of the Empire*, 1897, pay no regard to it. The simple explanation is that some copyist in transcribing MCCCCXCVII did not properly join the lines of the letter V, making them appear to be II. This would give XCIIII. But the date of the Letters Patent should put the matter beyond dispute.

Sir Robert Thorburn, in his tribute to Cabot, pays the following compliment to his neighbors of the United States:

Adown the mighty ages as we scan
The list of England's heroes in the van
Of honored names, Cabot will hold a place
Among the benefactors of the race
Whose flag today o'ershadows every sea,
Teaching the world the "birth-right of the free."

And did Columbia, our fair sister, too
Her virgin beauty spread before his view,
She who, what time her starry banners wave,
Leads forth the sons of "Pilgrim Fathers" brave.
O Cabot! own their common ancestry,
Sons of England! brothers of our race!
God bless and prosper ye with every grace,
Be ye the monument to Cabot's name
And write his record on a scroll of fame.

20

A Successful Business: Martin Bros.

"Martin Brothers," *Christmas Review*, 1897, 25

Despite the falling off in the volume of business generally in this city, it is gratifying to know that some firms are not only holding their own but are even increasing and extending their trade. This is especially the case with Messrs. Martin Brothers, the lumber and produce merchants whose premises are situated in Water Street, just west of Messrs. Job Bros. & Co. The firm consists of Messrs. Albert H. Martin and William J. Martin: the former has had extensive experience in the lumber business, the latter in produce; and their combined knowledge makes the secret of their success. A younger brother of the members of the firm – Mr. Michael Martin – is the bookkeeper of the business. He too has had considerable experience in this line, and no more suitable man could be procured for the position. The three brothers are all genial young men and are very popular, not only in the city of St. John's but throughout the Island wherever they are known. They are honest in all their dealings and might be recognized as the leading lumber and produce firm of the city.

Every year since the start, the volume of their trade has increased, and, no doubt, this will continue in the future. During the present season they landed over 3,000,000 feet of lumber, every inch of which was the product of local mills. This, of course, does not include shingles, of which they handled two and a half million. The lumber sold consists of plank, studding, joisting, plain and matched board, shingles, laths, palings &c. They always keep their stocks well up so that at any time during the year any stock that a carpenter may require he will find at Martin Brothers. During the summer months, Messrs. Martin give a great deal of employment to local schooners in bringing lumber from the mills, especially the mills of the northern bays, and from May to December their wharves are crowded with discharging vessels. The discharging, measuring, stowing &c. of the lumber give considerable employment, and the premises always present a busy appearance.

The lumber branch of the business is the special care of Mr. A.H. Martin, while the produce branch is more particularly looked after by Mr. William J. Martin. This branch of the business has also largely increased since it was started, and some of the largest and best produce men in Lower Canada now consign their goods to Messrs. Martin. Quite recently the firm have had to enlarge their premises to meet the growing demands of this branch of the trade, and it looks now as if they will soon want more. In this branch they handle hay, oats, potatoes, butter, meat, poultry &c. At present they have large stocks of meat and poultry, especially for the Christmas season, and there is no place in town where a better "bird' for the Christmas dinner can be procured. The past week two large cargoes of produce have arrived from P.E. Island to Messrs. Martin, and there are more on the way.

No other dealers in the same line in town will have anything like as large a stock as they will; and, as they will put nothing before their patrons but the freshest and best goods, they may anticipate a big trade. A visit to their stores and premises will make one wonder where purchasers are coming from for all the goods – piles of turkeys, stacks of geese and ducks and mountains of mutton, beef and pork. The stores are clean and cool, and purchasers can rely on getting a choice bird or quarter by purchasing it at Martin's.

21

Rugby or Kicking the Cod

"Rugby," *The Record*, January 1898, 14

During the past four or five years this game has advanced considerably in Newfoundland among football players, the different technical points of the game have been more looked into than formerly, and as a consequence, players seem to understand much more of the play and understand what they are acquainted with much better than in the past. The name Rugby Football is known here as "Kicking the Cod" and "Rushing the Waddock." In the past five years the St. John's team has only been beaten once, and that by the team composed of men from H.M.S. *Crescent* and other ships of the fleet here this season. They have played several matches with the warships, in which they have shown themselves quite able to take care of themselves and their reputation.

A great change has of late years taken place in the rules of this game, especially this last four or five years. As they now stand the referee is invested with full charge of the game, and so prevents any ungentlemanly or rough conduct that it is now almost impossible for a man to be hurt, that is if the rules of the game are properly followed. It is strange, even in Newfoundland, what a crowd of people will go to see a "rugby" match when they would not go a stone's throw to look at an association [football] game, owing probably to the larger amount of excitement which is attached to "rugby" than "association," and anything that is exciting is pretty sure to be enjoyed.

The forwards of the St. John's team do not, apparently, quite understand the right "heel" out and "screwing scrums" as yet, but no doubt with more practice they will yet become a fine lot of fellows. Of the "halves," of course T. McNeil stands out prominent as the best half in the country and a good all-round man at Association or Rugby. Some of the "three-quarters," especially Wearing Hayward and the "centre" Mars, are worthy [of] a place in some crack fifteen on the other side, while Goodridge, at full back, is a strong player, though young. The interest in this game is undoubtedly growing rapidly in Newfoundland, and if there was only a good enclosed ground available for matches there would be an opportunity to invite some of the Halifax teams to come and play here, but under present circumstances that is, of course, out of the question. Still we trust that in the near future this will be *fait accompli* and that we shall see matches played with many other teams than those the St. John's fifteen have now to depend on. This season, although never having any practice games – which in most all crack teams is, of course, carefully attended to – the St. John's men have done remarkably well when playing together. They have played H.M.S. *Cordelia* four times, all of which games they won. Then there was a match with a picked team from the fleet – *Crescent, Cordelia* and *Mohawk*, which they lost to a penalty kick to nil; but had the referee been perfectly clear in his decision and not had to appeal to players of the other side on the field, the game would in all probability have ended in a draw. From this out we hope to see "Rugby" make more rapid strides still and some good matches take place next season.

22

St. John's in 1899

Patrick Thomas McGrath (1868-1929) was born in St. John's and received his early education at the Christian Brothers' schools. In 1891, he began work as a reporter for the *Evening Herald* and was later Newfoundland correspondent for the *London Times*, as well as other newspapers and magazines in England, Canada and the United States.

P.T. McGrath, **"St. John's, Newfoundland,"**
Nash's Pall Mall Magazine, 18 (1899): 4-15

St. John's should possess a special interest for the British people on several grounds: it is the oldest settlement in North America, it is the chief town of their most ancient colonial possession, it is the spot where their adventurous ancestors first set foot when their daring spirit prompted them to seek new lands beyond the sea, it is the centre of the region which saw the beginnings of England's navy, it sheltered the men who scoured the Spanish Main, sank the Armada and carried "the meteor flag" [96] into every clime. Gilbert, Raleigh, Drake, Hawkins, Cook, Rodney and other noted figures in marine annals were associated with its early days.

The founding of St. John's dates back to the discovery of North America. Cabot, on his famous voyage, sighted the

Newfoundland coast and cast anchor in this harbour on June 24th, 1497, naming it after the saint whose feast-day it was. When he returned to England the tale of his discoveries and the wealth of the fisheries of "ye new isle" spread far and wide. Seven years later, in 1504, English ships were engaged in the fisheries, as were also caravels from France, Portugal and Spain, St. John's being their rendezvous. From the start the doughty Englishmen asserted their mastery over the island and all other nations resorting there. They built huts and fishing stations, hunted and trapped, and eventually made their home there. The fishery speedily became of first importance. Great convoys left the West Country every spring for St. John's, fished all summer and returned in the autumn with their garnered wealth of sea and shore. This was nearly a century before the mainland of America was effectively settled, Virginia plantation not being established till 1610, while the Pilgrim Fathers did not land on the Massachusetts coast till 1620.

Rapidly the colony grew, and on August 7th, 1583, Sir Humphrey Gilbert arrived at St. John's and took possession of the island for his royal mistress, Queen Elizabeth. By that time the harbour was known as a shelter port by every mariner who sailed the western ocean, and Gilbert, on entering, found forty sail of vessels in the harbour, English and foreign, who prepared to give him battle, until he sent in a boat to explain his mission, when, as the narrative states, "they caused to be discharged all the great ordnance of their fleet in token of our welcome." He was entertained most heartily by the English merchants at their homes and "summer garden," and his crews were surprised at the importance of the place. These fisherfolk were the class who afterwards broke the sea power of Spain and France and made England what it is today – the mistress of the world. That this contention is not far-fetched is proved by the fact that France uses the Newfoundland fisheries as a nursery for her navy down to this very day.

With the seventeenth century, pirates and sea-rovers made descents upon the town, and the Stuarts tried to extirpate the resident population. The infamous Star Chamber[97] parcelled out the settlements into plantations for court favourites and powerful companies who wished to keep the island as a mere fishing station. It was forbidden the people to winter here, to build permanent houses or to bring women into the island. "Justice" was administered by fishing admirals, the first captain arriving each year being admiral for the season, the second-vice-admiral and the third rear-admiral.

The town was captured by the Dutch admiral De Ruyter in1676, and three years later Charles II ordered the removal of the whole population from the soil. This barbarous edict was not put into force, however; but in 1697 the French, under D'Iberville, captured the town and burnt it, deporting to England every one of its people – 224 in all – who had survived the fighting and had not fled into the woods. The next year, Sir William Norris, with troops from England, restored it, leaving a garrison of 300 men, of whom 214 perished the following winter owing to the loss of a store-ship.

Another French expedition attacked it in 1705, burning the town but failing to capture the forts. Three years afterwards these succumbed to an expedition under St. Ovide;[98] but the French were driven out finally and the town rebuilt the following year.

These struggles attracted English administrative eyes to the colony; and as the little town had survived the proscriptions of the Stuarts and the horrors of war, a more enlightened policy was adopted and the rule of the fishing admirals was abolished, Captain Osborne, R.N.,[99] being appointed the first Governor in 1727, fifty years before Australia was discovered and thirty before Wolfe's victory at Quebec "gave England a continent."

For the last time the *fleur-de-lys* floated over St. John's in 1762, when [Avhen] D'Aubusson captured it with 1,500

Frenchmen; but Sir William Amherst speedily dislodged him, and the French fleet fled from the port, leaving the land forces prisoners in his hands.

The town was destroyed by fire in 1816, 1818, 1846 and 1892, the last of these conflagrations involving the loss of property to the value of £4,000,000, rendering 13,000 people homeless and reducing to ashes nearly all the principal public buildings and religious edifices. Commercial disaster likewise contributed its share to retard the growth of the town in 1814, 1860 and 1894, the last year being remarkable for the collapse of its two banks and many of its leading business houses. Religious intolerance also played its part, the Catholic religion being proscribed until 1784; and education was also discouraged, the town not attaining the dignity of a grammar school until 1799. St. John's now has a population of 30,000, all of British stock, the sons of English, Scotch and Irish emigrants who flocked there in the past, when it was the half-way house to the Western Hemisphere. They form a race of brave, hardy, generous people who, in their isolation, have preserved the noblest virtues of the race from which they sprang, unsullied by contact with the great world outside. This isolation – almost unique in English-speaking peoples – forms one of the great charms of the place for the visitor. The inhabitants are simple in their habits, frugal in their lives, daring and healthy from the very nature of the arduous avocations they pursue. They and their kindred have been fishermen for generations, the Viking blood is in them, and whether in their frail boats seeking for codfish off the coast or treading with undaunted spirit the yielding icefloes in the quest for seals, they are equally at home.

The harbour is entered through a gap in the beetling hills, seeming as if some fabled giant had cleft the fracture with a blow of his battle-axe. In these placid waters a mighty fleet could lie at anchor, undisturbed by the storms outside, and yet the entrance channel is deep enough to admit the largest ironclad afloat. The "Narrows" is about 500 feet wide, and the cliffs rise 700 feet high on either side, crowned with dismantled fortifications which we hope to see soon restored. In the "good old days" when French and English contended for its mastery, it was customary to provide against night attacks from sea by stretching a heavy chain across the "Narrows" each evening at sundown, and "Chain Rock" with its ringbolts and fastenings is still pointed out to visitors as a relic of the musty past.

The town is built on the northern hillside. It rises in regular tiers from the waterfront to the plateau above and overflows out to the charming valley of Freshwater, lying behind the hill. The south side of the harbour is devoted very largely to seal-oil refineries, and here are moored the fleet of powerful wooden steamers in which the seal-fishing is prosecuted. They are the staunchest ships in the world for ice-navigation, and they have taken every American polar expedition to the Arctic regions for the past thirty years. The town is chiefly remarkable for its splendid churches and kindred institutions. The Roman Catholic cathedral surmounts the crest of the hill and is visible many miles to sea. It is, with two exceptions, the largest church in North America; it holds 7,000 people and cost £120,000. The sister cathedral of the Anglican body was destroyed in the fire of 1892. It was the finest specimen of Gothic architecture in this hemisphere, the design of Sir Gilbert Scott,[100] and it cost £150,000. It was the pride of the city, and its loss is deplored by all.

They were generous in endowing their churches, these old colonists; and colleges, schools, halls and orphanages also uplift themselves to bear testimony to their liberality. St. John's is the seat of the Colonial Government, Newfoundland being the only British possession in North America which clung to its legislative independence and declined to merge its identity in the Canadian

Confederation. The public buildings which escaped are but few. Government House, the residence of the Governor, is a square, rambling stone structure set amid thick woods and surrounded by spacious grounds. The Colonial Building, where the Legislature meets and some of the public departments are housed, is remarkable for its handsome Ionic portico, and the grounds are now being converted into a splendid park [Bannerman Park]. The town is also the great business centre, the mart or depôt for the commerce of the island. Through the "Narrows" comes fully 90 per cent of the imports – food, clothing, necessaries and luxuries for the two hundred thousands who inhabit its three thousand miles of coastline, besides the lonely region of Labrador; and out of the same channel is borne as large a proportion of the exports – codfish, sealskins, oils, lobsters, salmon, etc. Every spring the harbour is crowded with hundreds of fishing craft from the coast settlements which have come to St. John's for the fishing outfit; and every fall they return again to barter their catch for the goods with which the merchants' stores are filled. St. John's owes its prosperity to codfish. As you enter the harbour you see the rude fishing stations on either side, with flakes, or platforms of poles and dried twigs on which the cod are spread to dry. The waterfront is lined with wharves at which are moored schooners with their catch and foreign-going vessels loading for market. The substantial warehouses behind are packed with codfish, and on a fine day wharves, rooftops, coves and all available spots are covered with the salt-encrusted staple export, drying in the sun. Water Street is the business thoroughfare where the island's commerce is controlled. It is lined with splendid shops where one may buy the finest fabrics or the most indispensable fishing requisites. The town does not yet boast the luxury of a paved street, though such a surface is about to be given this roadway during the summer, and an electric street-car service will be installed at the same time. From the town also starts the colony's railway system. This now includes a main or trunk line 550 miles long, piercing through the unexplored and uninhabited wilderness of the interior and terminating at Port-aux-Basques, the south-western extremity of the island, 90 miles from Cape Breton, to which the seventeen-knot ferry steamer *Bruce* runs, giving us daily communication with the American continent. There are also branch lines to other important centres, making a total of 650 miles in all.

The road through the island we expect to serve the purpose of making St. John's the link connecting the component parts of a new fast Atlantic steamship service. The distance from the Irish coast to St. John's is only 1,760 miles, about three-and-a-quarter days' run for the *Campania*, and this would be an immense reduction in the present lengthy sea voyage. Arriving here, the traveller would take the train across the country and thence be carried to any point in Canada or the United States, the saving of time effected being from twenty-four to thirty-six hours, not to speak of the discomforts avoided. The railroad also gives access to the unquestioned agricultural, timber and mineral resources of the island, by the development of which we set such store because they will serve to increase our population and better our conditions of existence.

The town forms the headquarters for all the mining and other industrial ventures undertaken. The country round it is rich in silver, copper, lead and iron; one hæmatite deposit at Bell Island, eighteen miles away, put out 200,000 tons of ore last season, and another is being worked at Western Bay under a guarantee of a minimum of 150,000 tons yearly.

With the recent discovery of coal in the interior, we anticipate an early establishment of smelting works near St. John's. Though the land round the city is held to be unequal to that in other portions of the island, agricultural possibilities are not insignificant. Hay, oats, barley, roots and garden produce are grown abundantly and the farmers are a well-to-do class, and the pursuit is becoming more popular every year.

But it is to the tourist, the sportsman and the artist that St. John's offers the chief attraction. If Nature has been churlish to us in other respects, she has made up for it by lavishly dowering our island with natural beauties. From the hills above the Narrows one has a seascape rarely equalled. The mighty ocean stretches away before your feet, unbroken by land until it reaches the Irish coast. Along the horizon floats the majestic procession of dazzling icebergs, a picture not possible elsewhere. Within a few miles of the city are typical Newfoundland fishing villages, perched in almost inaccessible coves and creeks, the delight of an artist's heart. Beautiful, smiling, well-tilled valleys and wooded hills strike the eye on every hand, and not a brook that runs but is filled with trout. In Quidi Vidi Lake, a pretty sheet of water nestling just behind the city and but ten minutes' walk from the business quarter, it is not infrequent to get trout weighing four to five pounds, while an hour's drive in any direction will ensure one a well-filled basket. If one would have more exciting fishing, a three hours' railway drive to Salmonier will bring him to the haunts of the salmon, and a run to the Humber River, the sporting ground of the island, will enable him to enjoy pleasures which not even the lease of a moor or salmon river in Scotland could afford him. Ptarmigan or partridge can be shot an hour's tramp from town, and splendid bags can be made after a four-hours' drive. Deer-stalking can be had which cannot be equalled in North America. All forms of sport are free, except caribou-shooting, for which a fee of £20 is exacted. As an illustration of the sporting possibilities of the island, I need only mention that on the Queen's birthday last year a trouters' train left this city with two hundred fishermen, who returned after twenty-four hours with over one thousand dozen of trout. As for deer-shooting, some seven hundred carcasses were brought to town last winter by the mail-boats in little over a month, shot by the settlers around the coast, and the meat sold here for three-half-pence a pound, and much of it was given to the poor.

From St. John's, steamers will take the traveller to any part of the island and to the Labrador peninsula; and the variety of beautiful scenery cannot fail to satisfy the most exacting. The fiords are said to surpass those of Norway, the beauty of the Humber and Exploits rivers is claimed to equal any in America, and the scenery of the Bay of Islands is the admiration of the hundreds of United States yachtsmen who have visited it. The social life of St. John's is a noteworthy feature. Each summer we have the British and French warships here, whose presence is necessitated by the famous "French Shore" Question.[101] These and the city people entertain largely; and, indeed, the hospitality of the townsfolk is proverbial. The wealthy classes, all of whom are educated in England, within a week's journey, combine the culture of the mother country with the colonial cordiality and open-heartedness.

We anticipate that before long the town will be again fortified by the imperial authorities. Its strategic importance cannot be exaggerated, dominating as it does the commerce of the North Atlantic, for most of the ocean steamers pass within a few miles of the harbour. Then it commands the water-borne trade of Canada, and if seized by an enemy and hastily fortified in wartime it would become a veritable thorn in England's side. It is naturally so suitable that to arm it would not be a serious undertaking, and British warships could lie securely within, ready to pounce out and sweep the ocean of an enemy's shipping. The discovery of coal in the island forms another reason why it should be made a military and naval base; then would follow the project of establishing a training ship here, where boys – the sons of fishermen – could be trained for the Royal Navy. Then St. John's would become what it was in the early days of its history, a nursery for seamen to carry Britain's banner over the seas and to uphold the Empire.

23

Progress Evident in 1899

H.F. Shortis Papers, *Provincial Archives*, vol. 4, 360-70

A single glance at its condition in 1799, the last year of the eighteenth century, will show what an advance has made in a hundred years. At that date St. John's contained a little over three thousand people, and they were huddled together in wretched wooden huts that were in constant danger of fire. There was but one house built of stone. Streets there were none. The houses were arranged along three parallel paths or "pats," as they called them in the vernacular, corresponding to Water St., Duckworth and Gower Streets of today. They were known as "the lower, middle and upper 'pats'." All were narrow, unpaved, unlighted and in every way abominable. The principal thoroughfare (what is now Water Street) was in one place not more than six feet wide.

We can hardly imagine what life was in those days, from which only two or three generations separate us. It was then the reign of the Naval Governors who strutted about and fumed and enforced quarter-deck discipline with stern rigidity. Their principal duty was to prevent settlement in the island and to take care that no land was enclosed or cultivated or used for purposes other than the fisheries. The population of the whole island was under twenty thousand. Roads there were none. Certain "pats" led out to the country and were used for hauling wood. In

Pokeham Path, Major's Path and others, we still have reminders of this period.

Admiral Waldegrave reigned in 1799. He was by no means a bad sort of governor, and the people certified their respect for his memory by naming a street after him – Waldegrave Street. It may be found near Riverhead and is certainly not a very flattering memorial. In those days, Governors kept their toes warm by returning to their own firesides in England on the approach of winter and returning when the snows disappeared. So did the Chief Justice, and the people got on as best they could without them and do not seem to have missed them very much.

In this very year of ninety-nine, one hundred years ago, Governor Waldegrave, before retiring to his winter quarters in England, issued strict orders to the High Sheriff, prohibiting the erection of buildings during his absence. On his return his wrath knew no bounds when he found that a Mrs. Gill, with woman's perversity, had actually put up a fence round a scrap of a garden and was going to plant potatoes and that two other audacious individuals had erected "sheds," having something suspiciously like chimneys. The Sheriff got an awful wigging from the irate Admiral and was ordered to take down fence and sheds immediately.

Ten years before, Governor Milbank[102] had discovered that a certain person had feloniously and of malice aforethought erected a house. In vain did he plead that it was only a covering for his potato cellar. The Governor went and made a careful scrutiny and found it had "a complete chimney if not two," and down it came; and with this came a notification that if any building were erected in future "except for the salting and curing of fish, it would be taken down" and that no private property in land could be allowed unless it was used for fishing purposes.

What a contrast does the St. John's of today [1899] present to that of one hundred years ago! It is a city of thirty thousand population. The old "pats" are streets, well sewered and lighted by electricity, with unlimited supplies of purest water. Water Street, a mile in length, is lined with handsome stores and shops, and Mr. Contractor [Robert G.] Reid is paving it with granite brought from the heart of the interior on a railway six hundred miles in length, and he is laying along the streets an iron track on which horseless, steamless cars luxuriously fitted up for passengers will be whirling, possibly before the twentieth century has drawn its first breath. Most wonderful of all, he will drive those cars by an invisible force [power station], which he will create at Petty Harbour, nine miles off, and his Ariel[103] will be a little brawling river that there tumbles into the sea. By the same viewless power he will drive the factories, printing presses and the whole machinery of St. John's if the services of his dainty Ariel are accepted; and also he will light the streets and houses and perhaps even cook the food for the people. Stately cathedrals and churches, handsome public buildings and dwelling houses now stand on the old "pats"; and on the summit of Signal Hill has been erected a memorial tower of imposing proportions to keep in honoured remembrance John Cabot, the discoverer of the Island.

If the old Admiral were to be permitted now to revisit the glimpses of the moon and look round him on the spot where he had the squabble with Mrs. Gill about the fence of the potato plot, how the irascible Governor would stare, if he did not swear, especially did the horseless cars come whirling past, disturbing all his ideas of the fitness of things. Not less amazing to him would be the great steamers entering the Narrows or taking their departure and the piercing shriek of the locomotive as it started for Port-aux-Basques with its long train of cars. Doubtless such a staunch Conservative, and true to the conditions of his time, would groan over these innovations and remark to himself, as he hurried back to the shades, "all this comes of allowing people to occupy land and erect houses with chimneys for other than fishing purposes. That impudent widow Gill set a bad example and has had too many followers. I wonder what has become of England's navy without its nursery in Newfoundland? Gone to pot, I suppose! Hello! What's that big house with ever so many chimneys? Government House, I declare! Well, the Governor has better times than I had, when I had to cross the Atlantic twice every year. My poor head is swimming at these changes – let me retire."

24

The New Electric Railway

R.F. Morkill was a railway engineer who later served in the Royal Flying Corps during the First World War.

R.F. Morkill, **"Our Street Railway System"**
Parsons' Christmas Annual, 1900, 12-13

Long distance transmission is at the present day one of the greatest engineering feats of the century. It has made wonderful strides within the last few years and is now so far developed that thousands of horse-power are sent over ærial wires for as long a distance as 150 miles, and that too with a very high efficiency However, there appears to be a limit to it, as with all other things.

For the first experiment at electrical transmission of power the Germans have credit. This was the Lauffen-Frankfort transmission, a distance of 110 miles, and took place in the year 1891. It was for the purpose of supplying power for the Frankfort Exhibition. The experiment proved a wonderful success, there being only the small loss of 26 per cent. Today America leads in electrical long distance transmission of energy. Every available water-power within reasonable distance of large communities is utilized for this purpose.

There are, of course, quite a number of different methods used in sending the power over the electrical wires, and the pressure varies with the distance transmitted. Much of the success is due to electrical street railroading, which has been making such rapid headway not only in America but in England and Europe. In order to make electrical railroading a financial success, cheap power must be available, and an abundance of it. Near coal-fields this is easily found; and now, with the art of utilizing water-power, electrical transmission is installed in many towns and cities far from coal-centres and where, without this great method of transmitting energy, it would be next to impossible to make it pay.

While in foreign countries, within the last seven or eight years, water-powers were being developed, electric railways installed and electric motors replacing the steam engines, St. John's was receiving no attention in this line, although it had a splendid water-power only eight miles away. It was not until Mr. R.G. Reid[104] got a franchise for an electric railway in the city that the people began to realize its importance. The introduction of the electric street railway naturally caused much wonderment, and the wonder grew when it was pointed out that the electric current not only had to find its way from the power-house over the trolley-wires and to the cars, wherever these may be, but it has also to return to the power-house through the track and ground.

Of the many different systems used in electrical propulsion are the third-rail system, which can only be used for elevated lines or when the track is securely guarded against pedestrians; the Conduit system, which is only an improved form of the third-rail system. The overhead trolley, although rather unsightly, certainly gives by far the best and most efficient results and is used almost entirely in America for surface roads.

In St. John's, on account of the exceedingly steep hills and narrow streets, which necessitate sharp curves, the engineers had many difficulties to contend with and have, with admirable success, surmounted all of them. The generating plant at Petty Harbor, eight miles from the city, is one of the most modern and improved that can be had. The water supply, of which there is an unlimited amount, is stored in several large ponds, known as the Petty Harbor Lakes, and is conveyed from the smallest pond to the generating station in a wooden flume eight feet square and 3,468 feet in length. It ends in a rock-tunnel 368 feet long and 187 feet above the station, at the other end of which is located the pen-stock. From this point an iron pipe, six feet six inches in diameter and 318 feet long, made of steel plates five-eighth inch thick, brings the water into the station at a pressure of eighty-eight pounds per square inch. This huge pipe is supported on twenty-two concrete pillars embedded in the solid rock. The water enters a large steel case in which is situated the turbine. This water-motor is known as the Victor type and is regulated for different loads by a bronze cylinder which projects around it and is run in and out according to the amount of water required by an electric governor, which works automatically. This water-wheel has a capacity of 1,868 horsepower.

On each side of the turbine case, connected by a steel shaft six and a half inches in diameter, are the generators, two in number. They have a rated capacity of 600 K.W. (800 H.P.) each and a speed of 327 revolutions per minute, giving a potential of 500 volts and sixty P.P.S. They are known as the Revolving Armature type. On a part of the shaft nearest the switchboard and between one of the generators and case is a nine-ton fly-wheel made up of sheeted steel, belted together and turned smooth in a lathe. This fly-wheel is to assist in governing. Tapped off from the side of the big pipe is a smaller one, supplying water to a small turbine quite similar in construction to the larger one. Its capacity is fifty H.P., and it drives two exciters arranged in the same manner. These two small direct-current machines are rated at 15 K.W. (18 H.P.) each; speed, 605 revolutions per minute;

generating current at a potential of 110 volts. They supply the necessary field current for the large alternators and also the lights for the power-house, and several arc lamps which have been erected in the streets at Petty Harbor.

The switchboard consists of four white marble panels: two for the generators and two for the exciters. On these are mounted the switches for controlling the current and the instruments for measuring the current and voltage. In order to successfully transmit the energy, 1,600 H.P., with as little loss as possible, the voltage has to be raised. This is done by means of three transformers, which raise the voltage to 15,000 volts, at which pressure the current is brought into the city. There are two pole lines. This is to ensure against any interruption of the service, as, if any accident occurs to one, the other can be immediately used without any interruption. On each pole line are three copper wires, so placed as to form an equilateral triangle. This makes a total mileage of copper of fifty-four miles. The wires have an area of 32,102 circular mils (No. 5 B. & S.). They are supported on twenty-five foot poles spaced 125 feet apart. On each pole are three glass insulators. This insulates the circuits from the ground and from each other.

Transmission wires enter the end of the sub-station. The current, after passing through high tension switches and circuit breaker, goes to four small transformers of 100 K.W. (125 H.P.), each to be again reduced to normal voltage (400 volts); also four large transformers of 150 K.W. (170 H.P.), each to reduce the potential to 2,040, which voltage is used for lighting and power throughout the city. The first set of smaller transformers are for rotary converters, or rotary transformers as they are sometimes called. These machines, of which there are two, transform the current from alternating to direct for street railway circuits. They have a rated capacity of 200 K.W. (250 H.P.) but will carry continuously twenty-five per cent overload without undue heating. Their speed is 720 revolutions per minute, generating at 500 volts pressure.

The switchboard consists of nine white marble panels, each panel four feet, four inches, two feet wide and two inches thick. Four panels are for rotary converters and one for railway feeders. The remaining four are for lighting and power. On the switchboard are mounted switches for controlling the current and meters for measuring the current and voltage.

The remaining interesting feature of the sub-station is that the Manhattan alternating enclosed arc system will be installed immediately for street lighting. This will necessitate the addition of one more panel to the switchboard. The feeders for railway light and power circuits make their exit directly above and behind the board to the city pole lines.

As stated above, the construction of the road required considerable engineering skill due to steep grades, narrow streets etc. On Holloway Street there is 120 feet tangent track with a grade of fourteen-and-a-half per cent and fifty-feet radius curve at top and bottom. This alone is a severe test on power apparatus. The track is narrow gauge, to be in keeping with the Newfoundland Railway, which has a gauge of three feet, six inches. Five miles of fifty-pound T rails have been laid, also 5,700 feet of eighty-three-pound girder rail on the principal street, which at present is being paved. The trolley wire is No. 00 and is suspended from poles on either side of the street.

Rails are bonded in the usual way and cross-bonded every 400 feet, No. 00 bonds being used for fifty-pound rails and 0000 for eighty-three pound. This bonding is done to increase the conductivity of the return circuit. It consists of connecting the rails together at joints by large copper wires. A hole is drilled near the end of the rail, in which is inserted one end of the copper wire. The end is trimmed to make a better electrical connection and then securely riveted to the rail, thus making a good, solid mechanical as well as electrical connection. In cross-bonding, the rails of one side are connected to the rails of the other side by copper wires, connections being made in the same manner as described above.

The rolling stock consists of six cars, thirty-two feet long, equipped with 12a thirty H.P. motors, series parallel, thirty-eight controllers, single trucks. On each axle is mounted a motor of thirty H.P. capacity. Four of the cars are double-enders: that is to say, they have controllers at both ends of the car and thus can be operated by the motorman either at the back or front. Two sweepers are ready for the winter season. They are propelled by two motors similar to the cars but have two extra motors of thirty H.P. capacity each for driving the brooms.

Besides the grade on Holloway Street, which has been previously mentioned, there are several others having grades of eight and ten per cent, and two or three curves of forty-five feet radius are also met with. As can be imagined, the cars, motors and trucks have had a pretty severe test, but notwithstanding that they have stood it admirably. All the electrical apparatus was manufactured by the Westinghouse Company and has given excellent satisfaction. The turbine and governor were manufactured by the Stillwell-Bierce Co., and the cars and trucks were made in Montreal, the former by the Larivière Car Mfg. Co. and the latter by the Montreal Switch Co. Mr. G.H. Massey is the consulting engineer, Mr. W.A. Mackay is superintendent and electrical engineer and Mr. F. H. Wing is electrical engineer in charge at Petty Harbor, and to these gentlemen is due the credit of building and operating this highly successful installation.

25

St. John's in 1900

P.T. McGrath, **"Newfoundland's Chief Town"**
Newfoundland Magazine, 1 (1900): 7-12

To the tourist, the sportsman, the artist, the health-seeker, the historical student or the blasé "globe-trotter," St. John's offers attractions which few cities combine in such a satisfactory manner. It is the capital of England's oldest colony. It is a centre whence can be reached in a few hours splendid streams and lakes which are the joy of anglers, grouse moors free to all, and caribou barrens where these noble deer are found in thousands. It abounds in scenes to inspire the artist's brush or pencil, the environs presenting every variety of picturesque scenery. Its salubrious climate in summer renders it an ideal location for the invalid. That France and England struggled for its mastery for nearly three centuries indicates that many incidents will be found in its history for that period well worth perpetuating in some historical record. Its remoteness and isolation make it an irresistible temptation to the sightseer in search of "fresh fields and pastures new"[105] who has even the crudest information as to its advantages in these respects.

Its early history is romantic in the extreme. Discovered by Cabot in 1497, its settlement may be said to have begun with the day he entered its harbour. The waters around the coast and the great submarine Banks, some seventy miles to sea, teemed with codfish, and ere many years English, French, Spanish and Portugese fishermen were making their way to this new region every spring, returning to their own ports in the autumn with their rich freights of fish, then of great value, especially in the Catholic countries. St. John's then meant Newfoundland, and for nearly a hundred years no European country claimed the place, though the English fishermen outnumbered all competitors, the French ranking next. In 1583 Sir Humphrey Gilbert set up Queen Elizabeth's standard in the port, in the presence of the fishing skippers of these several nations, and made formal proclamation that it was henceforth English territory. The authority of the Crown, however, was but nominal until well into the next century. By this time the fishery, as far as England was concerned, was centred in the hands of merchant-adventurers from the West Country, who fitted out and maintained large fleets of ships to engage in it. Apprehensive of competition, they secured the passage of laws dividing up the coast into plantations to be apportioned among them. The resident population, then a few hundred people, were ordered to be removed from the soil, and it was forbidden any person to winter on the island under pain of death. It was to be a mere summer fishing station; every ship master had to give bonds to bring back each autumn all the men he took out in the spring, and no women were to be taken there on any pretext. The captain of the first fishing vessel arriving was admiral for the season, the second was vice-admiral and the third rear-admiral, and this was the only judicial machinery provided by the English council for the maintenance of law and order among the thousands of fishermen.

The pirates and privateers of the period frequently harassed the town, and the changing fortunes of war saw it pass into different hands. De Ruyter, the famous Dutch sea-rover, took it in 1676, and though the English soon regained possession, it fell into the hands of D'Iberville, the French freebooter, in 1697. For the next twenty years it was a bone of contention between the two nations, the French having it one year and the English the next. Such a state of things caused constant irritation in England, and in 1727 it was decided to supply it with an adequate garrison, a naval captain named Osborne being appointed as the first governor. French aggression was thus stayed until 1762, when the French again made a descent upon it and captured the town and forts, but Sir William Amherst recovered it within a few months, since which time it has remained in the undisturbed possession of England.

During the American War of Independence, and again in 1812, the port was the rendezvous of the British fleets, and many a prize was brought in, and all through the stormy period when Napoleon was the great shadow over Europe it served a like purpose. At all times it was a shelter port for shipping in distress upon the Atlantic, and in the days prior to the laying of the Atlantic cable it was the centre from which the news of one continent was disseminated to the other. It is the most eastern town in the New World, and if the vision could be projected sufficiently far, an observer standing on the summit of the hills which enclose the harbour would see before him the sunny slopes of France, the mouth of the Loire, and the city of Nantes, which lie on the same parallel of longitude. Northward and nearer would stand out the green shores of Ireland, only one thousand, seven hundred and sixty miles away, a bare three days' run for a modern ocean greyhound. It is the dream of every Newfoundlander, and one by no means unlikely of realization, that in the near future the transatlantic passage will be made by way of Newfoundland. The ocean trip will be reduced to three days; the discomforts incident thereto will be minimized; and trains and ferries will hurry the traveller to his destination with the accompaniments of ease and luxury now lavished upon these vehicles of transportation. Forty years ago a line of steamers ran from Galway, on the west coast of Ireland, to St. John's, and while no means then existed for completing the trip by rail, the experiment served to show that here was the idea which some future genius should give concrete expression to by providing connecting lines of rail and steamers which would embody every improvement calculated to expedite travel between the two worlds.

St. John's stands today an eloquent testimony to the indomitable spirit of the Anglo-Saxon race. The fishing settlement of past centuries remained little better than that until the year 1800. Only then was a road built outside its limits; only then was a grammar school established; only then was the Catholic religion recognized. Misgovernment, oppression, injustice, intolerance – all failed to crush the spirit of the people, though the growth of the place was immeasurably retarded thereby. Disasters of various kinds all proved impotent in preventing its advancement. The town was four times devastated by fire in this century – in 1816, 1818, 1846 and 1892; but each time it was rebuilt on a larger and more pretentious scale. The fire of 1892 occasioned a loss of $20,000,000, only one-fourth of which was covered by insurance, and yet today the town is more substantially built and more prosperous than ever. Similarly, it withstood commercial collapse in 1816, 1840 and 1894, and likewise the ravages of cholera in 1854.

Today it boasts a population of thirty thousand, all of British stock, and a commerce unequalled for a town of its size. It is, as it were, the clearing-house for the whole island. The great fish merchants, descendants of those who originally controlled the industry, are established in St. John's, which is, indeed, practically the sole town in the colony. The fishery is directed from here; the fishermen obtain their outfits and barter their catch here; the dried cod are shipped to market from here; the annual seal hunt is prosecuted from here, and the oily harvest is handled at the city wharves. Almost all the colony's imports – food, clothing, fishing requisites, etc., – enter this port and are distributed to all the fishing hamlets around the coast, and every minor industry or factory is established within the city limits. Hence it is clear that it must be a busy, bustling commercial centre with active, keen-witted businessmen, hundreds of tradespeople and hosts of operatives, fishermen and laborers. When the sealing steamers are outfitting in the early days of March, during their return in April month, when the cod fishers arrive in May for their supplies, and during the fall when they return to "square up," the business centres are alive with stalwart fishermen, and hundreds of fishing schooners are at anchor in the harbor or discharging their fish at the merchants' wharves.

The churches, colleges and such like institutions are unusually fine for a city of this size, and probably nowhere is religion more zealously practised and education more sedulously promoted. The public buildings are equally creditable, for being the seat of the colonial government, all the important departments are housed here. Newfoundland has never joined the Canadian federation, and the British system of colonial autonomy is seen in all its completeness, if in miniature, in St. John's. In the harbor are the British warships which protect the fisheries, the governor is a British official and the Executive Ministry and two Houses of Parliament are modelled on their British prototypes.

Codfish is now ceasing to be the badge serving to identify St. John's. Though that industry still retains its early vigor and the ocean teems with as great an abundance of the lordly cod as in the days of Cabot, other avenues are opening up, and commercial enterprise finds an outlet in new directions. The building of a railway disclosed to us that we had a country of great latent wealth, and the coming of Mr. [Robert G.] Reid, the millionaire railway contractor of Montreal, enabled us to inaugurate the development of these resources. While twenty years since there was not a locomotive in the island, St. John's is now the centre of a railway system some six hundred miles in length, cutting the interior in two, traversing the mineral belts, the arable areas and the forest lands and bringing into close touch with the capital the remotest coast settlements. The railway tops the great bays north and south, which eat into the mass of the island. On these bays are steamers which connect with every hamlet, and there is daily communication between St. John's and every mile of the seaboard. Nor is this all. A fast steamer, the *Bruce*, forms the link between our railway system and that of the Intercolonial at North Sydney, Cape Breton, and daily traffic is thus maintained between the colony and all parts of Canada and the United States.

The completing of the railway and perfecting of these communications will enable St. John's shortly to take rank as a leading tourist resort. Hitherto its isolation was its chief drawback, but that has now been removed. Today the visitor can reach here as readily as he can any of the favorite and much-heralded regions of the western continent, while the variety and entertainment provided for him will be much greater. The city of Quebec is visited by thousands of tourists every summer, and St. John's has attractions not inferior to it. Here are to be seen old forts antedating those of that city. Every hill is crowned with its crumbling batteries, many a hard-fought battle was waged on the ground now given over to the grazer or husbandman in the environs, and relics of the French occupation are dug up with many an excavation. Nature in her most yielding mood has lavished upon the suburbs her most beautiful scenery, while every stream yields a bountiful basket of plump trout. A little farther away salmon may be got, sometimes reaching thirty pounds weight, and cod-catching with the hardy fishermen from the coves near the town is always to be had. The delights of grouse shooting or deer stalking are not to be told in the limited compass of this article, but it can safely be said that not even the most exacting sportsman need go away unsatisfied. The visitor to St. John's can make his plans to reach any part of the island he desires, can obtain guides and bearers at low rates and can enjoy every form of sport the island offers without any charge or limitation, save in the case of the caribou, where a license fee is exacted and the number to be killed is prescribed. From St. John's also can be reached the remote Labrador peninsula, the rugged, picturesque scenery of which will more than pay the visitor for his trip, not to speak of the pleasure afforded by the spectacle of the mighty icebergs floating southward from their Arctic homes, a feature of the marine panorama which is never absent during the summer months when the route would be open for tourist travel.

The future of St. John's cannot but be a successful one. The expansion of its commercial and trade relations is steadily increasing. The establishment of labor-giving industries grows apace. The mining, lumbering and pulp-making enterprises which are being set on foot in the interior will materially promote its prosperity, as it must be the depot whence their supplies will be drawn. Bell Island, eighteen miles distant, is the seat of the great hematite iron deposit from which the Dominion Steel Company obtains its stores of raw material for the smelting works at Sydney. Fully three thousand men are employed there this summer, and with such conditions reproduced in four or five different localities it is not difficult to realize what benefits must accrue to the metropolis. Tourist travel, too, is on the increase. To accommodate it a palatial hotel is being erected [the Newfoundland Hotel]. Other hotels will be built at suitable points along the railway line, and every facility will be provided for the comfort and entertainment of visitors. With the daily communication provided by the railway and *Bruce* service, the frequent steamer connections with Europe and America and the steamers skirting the coast and running to Labrador, there is every inducement for the tourist, while no portion of the island is beyond access by the sportsman. The British Admiralty will probably convert the port into a naval station ere long, fortifying it and providing a suitable garrison. One of the lessons of the existing war is that Great Britain needs more coaling stations along the great trade routes, and the strategic position of St. John's clearly points to it as being one of the ports to be used for such a purpose, particularly as it can be so easily defended and has the largest dry-dock in America. All these agencies will combine to enhance the city's prominence and welfare, to make it a greater attraction for strangers and to give it a recognized position among those coast-towns which play such a part in the maintenance of Britain's maritime supremacy.

Those of the leisured class can make no mistake in visiting St. John's. The people are kind-hearted, genial and hospitable, their pleasures are simple and their lives marked more by conflict with nature's obstacles than the carking cares of larger communities. The fishing villages, seemingly hundreds of years behind the times, are found but a mile or two from the city streets, and the electric trams will set one down at the fisher's cot, where a pair of dogs form the motive power for conveying his catch to market. No greater contrasts can be found anywhere, no more enticing scenes can tempt the sightseer, no more agreeable or interesting people can charm the visitor accustomed to hackneyed situations in this respect. From no region accessible at such small cost can the sportsman take away such a bag of game, and no recreation will prove as fruitful of benefit to the nerve-shaken dweller in great cities as a visit to St. John's.

Bibliography

Primary Sources

"Another Calamitous Fire at St. John's. Newfoundland," *Aberdeen Chronicle*, 20 December 1817, 2-3 [from the *Mercantile Journal,* 21 November].

Baird, John. "Short Account of the Rocks in the Neighbourhood of St. John's, Newfoundland," *Memoirs of the Wernerian Natural History Society*, 4 (1822): 151-56.

Benjamin, S.G.W. "A Summer Trip to Newfoundland," *Scribner's Monthly*, 2 (1871): 618-25.

[Brewster, Rev. John.] "Return of Prosperity After a General Fast," *Wesleyan Missionary Notices*, New Series 5, No. 105, September 1847.

"Curious Account of a Female Red Indian," *La Belle Assemblée; Or, Bell's Court and Fashionable Magazine*, 128, 1 October 1819.

Emerson, Hon. H.A. "Agricultural Improvement in Newfoundland," *Simmonds's Magazine*, 15 (1848): 393-94.

Fleming, Michael Anthony. "Catholic Mission of Newfoundland," *Weekly Orthodox Journal*, 1836, 201-5.

Howley, Michael Francis, "How Meagher Became a Millionaire: A True Story of Old St. John's," *Newfoundland Quarterly*, 4 (3), (1904): 2-3.

"A Hundred Years Ago," *Colonial Commerce*, 25 (1), (1915): 25-27.

LeMessurier, H.W. "How We Brought Out the *Morning Despatch,*" *Christmas Review*, 1892, 19.

-------. "Reminiscences of Old St. John's," *Newfoundland Quarterly*, 10 (3), 1910: 6-7.

"Martin Brothers," *Christmas Review*, 1897, 25.

McGrath, P.T. "St. John's, Newfoundland," Nash's Pall Mall Magazine," 18 (1899): 4-15.

------. "Newfoundland's Chief Town," *Newfoundland Magazine*, 1 (1900): 7-12.

Morkill, R.F. "Our Street Railway System," *Parsons' Christmas Annual*, 1900, 12-13.

"Newfoundland," *Lloyd's Evening Post*, 12-14 October 1796.

Pinsent, Sir Robert. "St. John's, Newfoundland, A.D., 1800-4," *Christmas Review*, 1892, 2-4.

Porter, Edward G. "The Cabot Celebrations of 1897," *New England Magazine*, 17 (1898): 653-71.

"Portia," "A Trip to Newfoundland," *The Week: A Journal for Men and Women*, 29 July 1886, 563-65.
"Rugby," *The Record,* January 1898, 14.
Shortis, H.F. "Random Jottings of By-gone Days," Papers of H.F. Shortis, Provincial Archives of Newfoundland and Labrador, vol. 2, 367.
-------. "Progress Evident in 1899," Papers of H.F. Shortis, Provincial Archives of Newfoundland and Labrador, vol. 4, 360-70.
-------. "How Criminals Were Punished in the Old Days," Papers of H.F. Shortis, Provincial Archives of Newfoundland and Labrador, vol.7, 84.
Wayback, Eros. "The St. John's Fire of July, '92," *Christmas Review*, 1892, 8.
Winton, A.C. "Newfoundland and Its Capital," *Dominion Illustrated Monthly*, 1 (1892): 657-66.

Secondary Sources

Beazley, Charles Raymond. *John and Sebastian Cabot: The Discovery of North America.* London: T.F. Unwin, 1898.
Dawson, Samuel Edward. "The Voyages of the Cabots in 1497 and 1498," *Trans. Royal Society of Canada*, 12 (1894): Sect. 2, 51-112.
Durnford, Mary, ed. *Family Recollections of Lieut.-General Elias Walker Durnford.* Montreal: Printed by John Lovell, 1863.
Harrisse, Henry. *Jean et Sébastien Cabot : leur origine et leurs voyages*. Paris: E. Leroux, 1882.
Harvey, Moses. "The Discoverer of North America and the First Colonizer of Newfoundland," *Maritime Monthly*, 4 (1874): 289-98.
Macpherson, Alan. G., ed. *Four Centuries and the City:Perspectives on the Historical Geography of St. John's.* St. John's: Dept. of Geography, Memorial University, 2005.
Marshall, Ingeborg. *A History and Ethnography of the Beothuk.* Montreal: McGill-Queen's University Press, 1996.
Moyles, R.G. *"Complaints is many and various, but the odd Divil likes it": Nineteenth Century Views of Newfoundland.* Toronto: Peter Martin Associates, 1977.
Weare, George Edward. *Cabot's Discovery of North America: The Dates Connected with the Voyage of the Matthew of Bristol.* Privately printed for the author, 1897.

Notes

1 Macpherson, 5.

2 Macpherson, 11.

3 For a summary of these events see "St. John's: A Century of Struggle" in R.G. Moyles, *"Complaints is any and various, but the odd Divil likes it"*, 1-30.

4 For a full account of farming in St. John's, see Robert MacKinnon, "The Agricultural Fringe of St. John's, 1750-1945," in Macpherson, op. cit., 53-81.

5 George Townshend, 1st Marquis Townshend (1724-1807), who reached the rank of field marshal.

6 Robert Pringle (d. 1793), military engineer sent to Newfoundland in 1772 to supervise the construction of defences around St. John's, as well as roads and bridges connecting them. Fort Townshend, Military Road and King's Road began under his direction in 1773.

7 Admiral Sir Charles Morice Pole (1757-1830).

8 Governor William Waldegrave (1753-1825).

9 Brigadier-General John Skerrett (1778-1814).

10 The Peace of Amiens, signed in 1802, marked the end of the French Revolutionary War.

11 Admiral James Gambier (1756-1833).

12 Dr. Edward Jenner (1749-1823) was an English country doctor who pioneered vaccination. He discovered in 1796 that inoculation with cowpox gave immunity to smallpox and saved countless lives.

13 Rev. Dr. John Clinch (1749-1819), a clergyman and physician regarded as being the first to practice vaccination in North America.

14 Lt.-Col. Thomas Skinner (1759-1818) was brought to Newfoundland in 1790 as Chief Engineer. He spent thirteen years in St. John's working on fortifications and other military matters.

15 Thomas Tremlett (1770-1830) became Chief Justice in 1803.

16 Letter-of-marque: a government license authorizing a private vessel to attack and capture enemy vessels and bring them before admiralty courts for condemnation and sale.

17 William Cull (fl. 1792-1823), fisherman, trapper, and lumberman.

18 Sir Erasmus Gower (1744-1815), Governor 1804-1806.

19 James Louis O'Donnel (c. 1737-1811), named Prefect Apostolic of Newfoundland in 1784.

20 Admiral Sir Richard Goodwin Keats (1757-1834) was a British naval officer who fought throughout the American Revolution, the French Revolutionary War and the Napoleonic War. He retired in 1812 and was made Governor of Newfoundland from 1813 to 1816.

21 See D.W. Prowse, *A History of Newfoundland from the English, Colonial and Foreign Records.* London: Macmillan and Co., 1895.

22 John William Hayward (1843-1913), amateur St. John's artist who depicted life in St. John's during the late 1800s.

23 Delft: a city in the province of South Holland, located between Rotterdam and The Hague. Delft is known for the painter Vermeer and Delft blue pottery.

24 Pierre Vergniaud (1753-1793) was a significant figure in the French Revolution.

25 The Rising of 1848: a failed Irish nationalist uprising led by the Young Ireland movement. It took place on 29 July 1848 in the village of Ballingary, Tipperary.

26 Mary Durnford, ed., *Family Recollections of Lieut.-General Elias Walker Durnford.* Montreal: Printed by John Lovell, 1863.

27 Jeffery Amherst (1717-1797), best known as one of the victors of the French and Indian War, when he conquered Louisbourg, Quebec City and Montreal. He was also the first British Governor General in the territories that eventually became Canada.

28 Henry Fox (1705-1774), British statesman.

29 Étienne-François, comte de Stainville, duc de Choiseul (1719-1785), French military officer, diplomat and statesman. From 1758 to 1761 and from 1766 to 1770, he was Foreign Minister and influenced France's global strategy.

30 During the siege of San Sebastián (7 July - 8 September 1813), allied forces from the army of the Duke of Wellington captured the city of San Sebastián, in northern Spain, from its French garrison.

31 Edward Augustus, Duke of Kent and Strathern (1767-1820), fourth son of George III and father of Queen Victoria. In the army, he served at Gibraltar, Canada, and the West Indies.

32 David Buchan (1780-c.1838): Scottish naval officer and Arctic explorer. From about 1808 to 1817, he operated in and around Newfoundland. He was the leader of an 1810 expedition into the interior of Newfoundland to attempt to make contact with the Beothuk and was appointed High Sheriff from 1825 to 1835.

33 Lionel Chancey (1748-1822), schoolmaster, born in Devon.

34 The Benevolent Irish Society was founded in 1805 by James McBraide, who was not himself a Roman Catholic.

35 Fridtjof Nansen (1861-1930), Norwegian explorer, scientist, diplomat, humanitarian and Nobel laureate.

36 Rev. Alexander FitzGerald was born in Ireland c.1770, and as a young man he joined the Dominicans. Arriving in Newfoundland in 1816, he was appointed curate to Bishop Thomas Scallon and several other priests from the Old Chapel on what is now Henry Street.

37 Sir Robert John Pinsent (1834-1893), named to the Supreme Court in 1880.

38 Faction fights: Organised fights between opposing factions, a feature of early nineteenth-century Ireland. They usually took place at fairs or other meeting places when drink was in abundance. The tradition is reputed to have begun in Tipperary in 1805.

39 Caesar Colclough (d. 1832), born in Ireland, was appointed Chief Justice in 1812, succeeding Thomas Tremblett.

40 John Kent (1805-1872), born in Ireland, was Prime Minister from 1859 to 1861.

41 Edward Patrick Morris (1859-1935) was Minister of Justice and Attorney General, 1900-07, and Prime Minister, 1909-18.

42 Dr. Willliam Carson (1770-1843), born in Scotland, was the garrison physician in St. John's, 1808-14, and Speaker of the House of Assembly, 1837-40.

43 The fisherman has been identified as William Cull of Fogo, 1803-1804. See Ingeborg Marchall, *A History and Ethnology of the Beothuk,* 129-32.

44 Henry John Boulton (1790-1870), Chief Justice of the Supreme Court from 1833 to1838.

45 Admiral Sir Henry Prescott (1783-1874), Governor of Newfoundland from 1834 to 1841.

46 Psalm 45: 1: My heart is inditing a good matter: I speak of the things which I have made touching the king: my tongue is the pen of a ready writer.

47 See *Methodist Hymnal*, 1889.

48 Psalm 122: 7: Peace be within they walls, and prosperity within they palaces.

49 General Sir John Gaspard Le Marchant (1803-1874), British army officer and Governor of Newfoundland from 1847 to 1852.

50 1 Kings 21: 29: Seest thou how Ahab humbleth himself before me? Because he humbleth himself before me, I will not bring evil in his days: but in his son's days will I bring the evil upon his house.

51 James Thompson, "Spring" (1729), 64-65.

52 The Dreadnought was the predominant twentieth-century battleship. The first of its kind, the Royal Navy's *Dreadnought*, had such an impact when launched in 1906 that battleships built thereafter were referred to as "dreadnoughts."

53 Phlebotomy: obtaining blood from a vein, in former days by incising a vein and letting the blood flow into a container.

54 Shortis was born in 1855.

55 The Crimean War (1853-1856): a conflict fought between the Russian Empire and an alliance of the French Empire, the British Empire, the Ottoman Empire, the Kingdom of Sardinia, and the Duchy of Nassau. Most of the conflict took place on the Crimean Peninsula.

56 Kenneth McLea (1800-1862), Scottish-born merchant who withdrew his candidacy as a Conservative in St. John's West in 1861 after a riot damaged his premises.

57 Lord Byron to Mr. Hodgson, 6 August 1809: "Seville is a fine town, and the Sierra Morena, part of which we crossed, a very sufficient mountain; but damn description, it is always disgusting.

58 Gut: a narrow passage of water.

59 Pilot-bread: hard tack, a simple type of biscuit made from flour, water, and sometimes salt. It was used, in the absence of perishable foods, during long sea voyages.

60 *Reliques of Ancient English Poetry* (sometimes known as Percy's *Reliques*) a collection of ballads and popular songs collected by Thomas Percy (1729-1811) and published in 1765.

61 "My Mind to Me a Kingdom Is," by Sir Edward Dyer (1540-1607).

62 Horace Bushnell (1802-1876), American Congregational clergyman and theologian.

63 Robert Dale Owen (1801-1877), born in Glasgow, Scotland, emigrated to the United States in 1825 and helped his father create the Utopian community of New Harmony, Indiana.

64 Pandemonium: the capital of Hell in John Milton's *Paradise Lost*.

65 William Kidd (1645-1701), Scottish sailor remembered for his trial and execution for piracy after returning from a voyage to the Indian Ocean.

66 Don Quixote: the main character of a novel written by Miguel de Cervantes and published in two volumes in 1605 and 1615.

67 Alloway Kirk: a ruin in Alloway, South Ayrshire, Scotland, celebrated as the scene of the witches' dance in the poem "Tam o' Shanter," by Robert Burns.

68 Southron: a person who lives in the South.

69 From a song attributed to J. Haskin, "We'll go to Sea No More": "Give me the field that no man ploughs/The farm that pays no fee."

70 Truck system: an arrangement whereby employees are paid in commodities or some currency substitute rather than money, thus limiting the employees' ability to choose how to spend their earnings.

71 William Shakespeare, *The Tempest*, 1.2: 229.

72 Tammany Hall, founded in 1789 as the Tammany Society, was the Democratic Party political machine that played a major role in controlling New York City politics and helping immigrants, most notably the Irish, to rise up in American politics from the 1790s to the 1960s.

73 George Thomas Rendell (1826-1909), merchant and member of the Legislative Council. While his house was saved, the fire destroyed his premises on Water St. He was subsequently a member of the Relief Committee formed to assist those left homeless.

74 Quebec Conference: the second meeting, held in 1864, to discuss Canadian confederation. The 16 delegates from the Province of Canada, Nova Scotia, New Brunswick, and Prince Edward Island had agreed at the close of the Charlottetown Conference to meet again at Quebec City. Newfoundland sent two observers but did not participate directly.

75 Ecclesiastes 11: 1: Cast thy bread upon the waters: for thou shalt find it after may days.

76 Pie: a confused mass of printer's type.

77 Printer's devil: assistant in a printing office.

78 Chase: an iron frame holding composed type.

79 Hon. Moses Monroe (1842-1895) was born in Moira, Northern Ireland, and came to Newfoundland in 1860. After working as a clerk, he started his own fishery supply business and later was associated with the establishment of several other businesses. In 1884, he was appointed to the Legislative Council

80 Ruby: a size of type.

81 Richard Eden (c.1520-1576), alchemist and translator. His translations of the geographic works of other writers helped foster a spirit of overseas exploration in Tudor England.

82 George Beste (d. 1584?), navigator who accompanied Frobisher on voyages of discovery for the North-West Passage.

83 Peter Martyr d'Anghiera (1457-1526), an Italian-born historian of Spain and its discoveries during the Age of Exploration.

84 Giovanni Battista Ramusio (1485-1557, Italian geographer and travel writer.

85 Richard Hakluyt (c. 1552-1616), English writer principally remembered for promoting the settlement of North America, notably through *Divers Voyages Touching the Discoverie of America* (1582) and *The Principal Navigations, Voiages, Traffiques and Discoueries of the English Nation* (1589-1600).

86 See Henry Harrisse, *Jean et Sébastien Cabot : leur origine et leurs voyages*. Paris: E. Leroux, 1882.

87 See Moses Harvey, "The Discoverer of North America and the First Colonizer of Newfoundland," *Maritime Monthly*, 4 (1874): 289-98.

88 Sir John George Bourinot (1836-1902), Canadian journalist, historian, and civil servant, a founding member of the Royal Society of Canada.

89 Samuel Edward Dawson, "The Voyages of the Cabots in 1497 and 1498," *Trans. Royal Society of Canada,* 12 (1894): Sect. 2, 51-112.

90 Cornelius O'Brien (1843-1906), appointed Archbishop of Halifax in 1882. From 1896 to 1897, he was President of the Royal Society of Canada.

91 William Wilfred Campbell (1858-1918), Canadian poet.

92 Sir Robert Thorburn (1836-1906) Newfoundland merchant and politician who served as Premier from 1885 to 1889. From 1870 to 1885 and from 1893 to 1906 he was also a member of the colony's Legislative Council.

93 Henry Harrisse (1829-1910). Born in Paris, he accompanied his family to the United States, where he became a lawyer. He returned to Paris and in 1897 entered the controversy on the Cabot landing.

94 George Edward Weare, *Cabot's Discovery of North America: The Dates Connected with the Voyage of the Matthew of Bristol.* Privately printed for the author, 1897.

95 Charles Raymond Beazley, *John and Sebastian Cabot: The Discovery of North America.* London: T.F. Unwin, 1898.

96 Meteor Flag: nickname for the version of the British red ensign in service from 1707 to 1801. The Meteor Flag was primarily a war ensign.

97 Star Chamber: an English court of law that sat at the Palace of Westminster until 1641.

98 Joseph de St. Ovide, Monbeton de Brouillan (1676-1755), the longest serving Governor of Isle Royal, 1717-1739.

99 Henry Osborn (1694-1771).

100 Sir George Gilbert Scott (1811-1878), English architect chiefly associated with the design, building and renovation of churches, cathedrals and workhouses.

101 French Shore: the French Treaty Shore came into existence with the ratification of the Treaty of Utrecht (1713), providing the French with the right to fish principally on the West Coast.

102 Mark Milbanke (1724-1805), Governor from 1789 to 1791.

103 Ariel: an archangel in Jewish and Christian mysticism, presented as an authority over the Earth and its elements.

104 Robert Gillespie Reid (1842-1908), born at Coupar Angus, Perthshire, Scotland.

105 John Milton, "Lycidas" (1637), 192-93: "At last he rose, and twitched his mantle blue: Tomorrow to fresh woods, and pastures new."

Ronald Rompkey is an University Research Professor in the Department of English at Memorial University.